Advaita Metaphysics

Contemporary Researches in Hindu Philosophy & Religion

(ISSN 0971-9628)

1. Idealistic Thought in Indian Philosophy; by Shuchita C. Divatia (ISBN 978-81-246-0021-4)
2. Karma and Reincarnation: The Vedāntic Perspective; by Muni Narayana Prasad (ISBN 978-81-246-0022-1)
3. Stonemill and Bhakti: From the Devotion of Peasant Women to the Philosophy of Swamies; by Guy Poitevin and Hema Rairkar (ISBN 978-81-246-0059-7)
4. Śaivism: Some Glimpses; by G.V. Tagare (ISBN 978-81-246-0076-4)
5. Advaita: A Conceptual Analysis; by A. Ramamurty (ISBN 978-81-246-0067-2)
6. Mind-Body Dualism: A Philosophic Investigation; by Alpana Chakraborty (ISBN 978-81-246-0071-9)
7. Hinduism and Scientific Quest; by T.R.R. Iyengar (ISBN 978-81-246-0077-1)
8. Indra and Other Vedic Deities — A Euhemeristic Study; by Uma Chakravarty (ISBN 978-81-246-0080-1)
9. Brahma-Vāda: Doctrine of Śrī Vallabhācārya; by G.V. Tagare (ISBN 978-81-246-0112-9)
10. The Science of Enlightenment: Enlightenment, Liberation and God — A Scientific Explanation; by Nitin Trasi (ISBN 978-81-246-0130-3)
11. Retrieving Sāṁkhya History: An Ascent from Dawn to Meridian; by Lallanji Gopal (ISBN 978-81-246-0143-3)
12. The Philosophical Foundations of Hinduism; by A. Ramamurty (ISBN 978-81-246-0163-1)
13. The Eternal Hinduism; by Baidyanath Saraswati (ISBN 978-81-246-0249-2)
14. Vedānta and its Philosophical Development; by A. Ramamurty (ISBN 978-81-246-0347-5)
15. Sāṁkhya-Yoga Epistomology; by Mukta Biswas (ISBN 978-81-246-0371-0)
16. A Sourcebook of Classical Hindu Thought; by Arvind Sharma (ISBN 978-81-246-0643-8)
17. A Treatise on Advaita Vedānta; by S. Bhuvaneshwari (ISBN 13: 978-81-246-0707-7)

Contemporary Researches in Hindu Philosophy & Religion, no. 18

Advaita Metaphysics

– A Contemporary Perspective –

Tapti Maitra

Indian Council of Philosophical Research
New Delhi

D.K. PRINTWORLD
Publishers of Indian Traditions

Cataloging in Publication Data — DK
[Courtesy: D.K. Agencies (P) Ltd. <docinfo@dkagencies.com>]

Maitra, Tapti, 1938-
Advaita metaphysics : a contemporary perspective / Tapti Maitra.
p. cm. (Contemporary researches in Hindu philosophy & religion ; no. 18).
Includes bibliographical references (p.).
ISBN 13: 9788124607473

1. Advaita. I. Title. II. Series : Contemporary researches in Hindu philosophy & religion ; no. 18.

DDC 181.482 23

ISBN 13: 978-81-246-0747-3
First published in India, 2014 Print run : 550 copies

Published by:
INDIAN COUNCIL OF PHILOSOPHICAL RESEARCH
Darshan Bhawan, 36 Tughlakabad Institutional Area
Mehrauli Badarpur Road, New Delhi - 110 062

and

D.K. PRINTWORLD (P) LTD.
Regd. Office: "Vedaśrī", F-395, Sudarshan Park
(Metro Station: Ramesh Nagar), New Delhi – 110 015
Phones: (011) 2545 3975, 2546 6019; *Fax*: (011) 2546 5926
e-mail: indology@dkprintworld.com
Website: www.dkprintworld.com

Printed by : D.K. Printworld (P) Ltd. New Delhi

Prologue

THE Upaniṣads are the earliest philosophical texts of the world. Profundity of a philosophical classic consists in the extent to which it tends itself to alternative interpretations. Needless to say that the Upaniṣadic texts have been viewed differently by commentators (*bhāṣyakāra*) down the centuries, of which the monistic interpretation of Upaniṣadic metaphysics by Śaṅkarācārya stands out conspicuous. An intimate reflection on the varied interpretations brings home the fact that, by and large, thinkers and scholars have read their native presuppositions and mystical convictions into the Upaniṣadic texts. Ontology is construed as basic and fundamental. Logic, epistemology and ethics therein are thought to be parasitic on metaphysics. There are a host of contemporary thinkers like G.R. Malkani, K.S. Murty and many other scholars who offer alternative perspectives and novel vistas to find new inroads into understanding the doctrine of Upaniṣads. *Tarkapāda Bhāṣya* is a significant exercise to spell out the logical system embedded in the text.

While adjudging the coherence and adequacy of classical interpretation, I have examined at length how logic and epistemology stand out as fundamental and can constitute as a starting point of excursion to the understanding of Advaita metaphysics. I have undertaken a faithful analysis of Advaitic logic and epistemology which provides a secure basis to the monism of Upaniṣads, as revealed in the notion of *Brahman* or *Ātman*.

The central theme of the proposed work is the exposition of the formulation of the Advaita theory of monism on the basis of epistemological and logical analysis of knowledge in *Adhyāsa Bhāṣya*. I have argued how the Advaita system is essentially a logical enterprise and seeks to eliminate speculative or metaphysical ideas. I have addressed the fundamental questions of Advaita enterprise as a prelude to the interpretation of *Vedānta-Sūtra*. Śaṅkara elaborately discusses the structure and limits of human knowledge and pointed out the perpetual logical error involved in the judgemental knowledge expressed in the propositional form. Consequently, Śaṅkara denounces the validity of factual knowledge and elucidates the nature of true knowledge bereft of any description whatsoever. This kind of knowledge has been characterized as Truth and ultimate Reality. These twin ideas represent the concept of *Brahman*.

Śaṅkara had demonstrated the method of elimination of factual knowledge and has pleaded in favour of a method of acquiring valid knowledge (*pāramārthika jñāna*). With the prefatory demonstration of Śaṅkara's philosophical investigation, I have proceeded to unearth the logical foundation of Advaita metaphysics spelt out in the research works of some eminent Advaita scholars.

I have subjected G.R. Malkani's review of Advaita metaphysical concepts as well as Advaita methodology to critical scrutiny. His philosophical work deals with the principal tenets of Advaita metaphysics, elucidating the doctrine of monism with its accompanying characteristics. The characteristic feature of the treatment of the subject has been underlined.

Malkani offers a rational interpretation of the traditional thinkers in consonance with scriptural statements. In course of his exposition of Indian spiritualism, he seeks to do away with the mystical underpinnings. He has brought out the theory of spiritualism of Advaitins by rational and logical arguments. He moots the thesis that spiritualism is an integral part of human life and idealism does not connote any set-ideal beyond human aspirations. In this context, Malkani has illustrated the social applicability of supreme value, i.e. *ānanda*. Accordingly, his philosophical review reconciles Advaita philosophy with Advaita theory of religion and morality. In his exposition of Advaitism and religion, Malkani has made a remarkable contribution in viewing Advaitism as "the religion of knowledge". According to him, the doctrine of Absolutism is the meeting point of religion and philosophy. He defines Advaitism as synthesis of philosophy and religion.

Malkani pleads in favour of a special type of Ādvaita methodology, viz., supernormal method. I have attempted to show that the word "supernormal" does not denote any supersensible element. He has explained the meaning of revealed words — *śabda*, *śruti*, etc. — under the rubric of supernormal method for acquiring the knowledge of *Brahman* (*brahma-vidyā*). While narrating the course of supernormal method, Malkani is explicit in expounding spiritualism as the concept of *ānanda*, the essential part of the definition of *Brahman*. He has underlined the role of *ānanda* in organizing all modes of human activities for the attainment of highest goal, i.e. *mokṣa*, the supreme value. Further, he has emphasized that the "supreme value" is a social value which can be achieved in this life cycle through cultivation of spiritual discipline. This introduces a new dimension in applied philosophy.

K.S. Murty is a prolific writer on various facets of philosophy. In the proposed project, I have confined myself to Murty's interpretation of the central metaphysical concept of Absolute/*Brahman*, substantiated by philosophical method. The salient features of his celebrated work on Advaita Vedānta, *Revelation and Reason in Advaita Vedānta* have been brought into bold relief. Murty's criticism of Advaita monism reveals a unique perspective to understand the monism of Advaita. I have sought to give proper estimation of his critique of non-dualism and logical definition of *Brahman*, illustrated by him; my chief concern is to present Murty's analysis of the Upaniṣadic definition of *Brahman*, viz. *satyam, jñānam* and *anantam*.

After the assessment of Murty's analysis of the metaphysical idea, I have set out for reviewing the methodological concepts, viz. reason and revelation. Murty has not discarded the role of reason in the Advaita method. Rather, "reason" acts as a subordinate means in the act of revelation of God as well as in acquiring the knowledge of *Brahman*. Accordingly, the notion of "revelation" has been treated as a higher type of knowledge. Revelation surpasses human reason but does not contradict it. He has rightly pointed out that higher knowledge is not incompatible with reason and logic. Moreover, man can distinguish between higher knowledge and lower knowledge by virtue of his rational faculty. Consequently, Murty clarifies that there is compatibility between higher knowledge and the rational or logical. Thus Murty effects a compromise in the last part of his book, mentioned above.

Murty adduces polemics against Advaita monism while expounding the "revelation of *Brahman*". He explains that revelation involves of dual concepts — the revealer and the revealed. This duality vitiates the doctrine of oneness of *Brahman*. He appeals to the scriptural statements to fortify the thesis of non-dualism. Murty argues from logical standpoint and refutes the concept of non-dual *Brahman* because of the dual activity involved in the process of revelation. This seminal point has been addressed with rigour and I construe it to be the major contribution of Murty, in his review of Advaitism.

I have sought to discuss and evaluate G. Misra's reinterpretation of Advaita system, especially the reconstruction of Advaita metaphysics by applying the analytical technique. Misra is the first Indian to pronounce boldly that Śaṅkara is not a dogmatic philosopher but a linguistic philosopher. Misra's philosophical enterprise has been solely concentrated on linguistic philosophy. He applies the method of linguistic analysis to resolve philosophical problems and issues in Advaita philosophy.

I have addressed myself to the basic features of Misra's evaluation on Śaṅkara's philosophical programme and discussed the major aspects of Misra's work on Advaita Vedānta. Misra confines himself to the theory of logic and language in his deliberation of Advaita theory of metaphysical essence. Misra has examined all the logical arguments of Śaṅkara to show that Advaita theory of Reality is based on the analysis of the nature and function of language and descriptive discourse. He has sought to show that *adhyāsa* (erroneous judgement) involves due to the application of attributive word to the subject, *aham* (the symbolic expression of *Ātman*). He contends that *Ātman/Brahman* cannot be represented in language or expressed in proposition because all propositional forms involve logical mistake. He elucidates how all empirical judgements combine two different types of concepts and thereby violate logical principle.

Misra's analysis of meaning-rules and language brings out the essential feature of the theory of language in Advaita philosophy. He has demonstrated how according to Śaṅkara, descriptive language, by its very nature, can never be complete in independent usage. Because of this incompleteness of meaning of descriptive words, Śaṅkara prefers demonstrative symbols without descriptive features, such as *aham, idam* and *tat* (I, this, that) as the basic concepts of Advaita metaphysics.

In his discourse on Advaita metaphysics, Misra has offered an extensive account of analytic philosophers like Russell, Wittgenstein and Strawson. In this part of discussion, Misra underlines the supremacy of Advaita system by comparing the Absolutism of Bradley.

I have also examined Misra's views on epistemological problems. He has defended Śaṅkara's arguments against perceptual knowledge because of the possibility of mis-description and misapplication of concepts in perceptual statements. He has elaborated various kinds of problems of perception in the illustration of the concept of *adhyāsa*.

Finally, Misra has sought to explicate how Śaṅkara formulated the logical doctrine of metaphysical essence, *Brahman*, discarding descriptive language. Besides, he has elucidated how Śaṅkara pleads in favour of the idea of non-qualified existence, non-qualified experience and non-qualified bliss as the ultimate concepts, because all these ideas have built-in sense of logical certainty. In this context, Misra claims that Śaṅkara has analysed the meaning of pure existence, pure consciousness and pure bliss (*sat–cit–ānanda*) as the formal properties, which are integral to the fundamental concept, *Brahman* or the Absolute.

Epilogue : In this section I have given a synoptic evaluation of salient points addressed in the preceding chapters. In a nutshell, I have sought to summarize and review all that have been discussed so as to make this work accessible to scholars at large.

To compute the principal ideas of this research programme, I can only say that I have attempted to understand the Advaitavāda of Śaṅkara from a contemporary perspective. My endeavour has been to reveal the academic excellence of the different types of models of interpretation in distinctive ways. To excel the excellence further, I would like to add a few lines on the novelty of the constructive interpretation of K.C. Bhattacharyya. Bhattacharyya's name is not widely known because of abstruse expression of his views on Vedānta. Scholars like T.R.V. Murty and G.R. Malkani have been profoundly influenced by the original thinking of K.C. Bhattacharyya and acknowledge his unique creativity in relating classical German philosophy to the key issues of Advaita Vedānta. However, as a research worker, I find a new trend in Bhattacharyya's constructive interpretation of Vedānta. I mention only the seminal points of his constructive interpretation.

Bhattacharyya undertakes constructive interpretation of Vedānta. He does not take recourse to speculate it but aims at analytical interpretation of it. To begin with his constructive interpretation, Bhattacharyya has not elaborated what does he really mean by constructive interpretation. However, constructive interpretation may mean the following:

1. It may mean digging out an idea which was there in the germinal form in the original Vedānta but it has escaped the attention of subsequent commentators and scholars, for some reason or other. In such case, simply reconstruction would have been the befitting term for such a scholastic exercise. Further, in any act of interpretation the interpreter invariably interpolates some new meanings into the theme; otherwise this cannot be treated as an interpretation. To the extent an interpretation is an extrapolation of a new meaning, it is not an interpretation but a new creation.
2. Constructive interpretation may mean a kind of "sympathetic" interpretation as opposed to destructive interpretation. In such a kind of interpretation the interpreter replaces the original views of the author by his own views. However, it appears that Bhattacharyya in his constructive interpretation does not go beyond the traditional views on Vedānta that

> it is a system of religion. The only difference is that the Westerners treated Vedānta as a kind of cosmogony – a theory of creation without offering any logic and reason. Whereas Bhattacharyya argues that Vedāntic views are based on logic and reason. However, he does not cite any instance of "logic and reason" that the Vedānta espouses.

Now coming to his view that the central theme of Vedānta is *sādhanā*, this is really problematic. *Sādhanā* stands for a way of realizing God or the Absolute. Throughout the ages saints from various traditions have tried to practise the path of *sādhanā*. The names of Ramaṇa Maharṣi and some other saints may be mentioned in this connection. There are surely some illusive cases among the so-called *sādhaka*s but the fact remains that there are some genuine saints. There is no contradiction in thinking that there are such people and they are distinct in many ways from the common run of mankind and human history bears ample testimony to it. But philosophy is an academic discipline having its objective method and technique. Our world has produced many distinct and distinguished philosophers but we do not know if such philosophers were saints as well by any stretch of imagination. On the contrary, the world has produced many illiterate saints. Maybe, some ancient Indian philosophers apart from being great logicians and metaphysicians were engaged in *sādhanā*. But this will be too much to conclude that the central theme of Vedānta is *sādhanā*. This view or the constructive interpretation of Vedānta is not in consonance with the spirit of Vedānta as well as Indian philosophy.

Lastly, Bhattacharyya claims that Vedānta has greatly influenced Hinduism as a religion. Many scholars subscribe to such a view. Historically speaking, not only in India but also across the world, philosophical systems and religions have very often influenced each other. Hinduism is not a monolithic religion nor does it signify any essential feature. There are strands of Hinduism. There are theist as well as atheist Hindus. What is significant is that the gods or deities in the Vedic pantheon are anthropomorphically conceived, whereas in the Vedāntic text, the highest reality has been conceived as impersonal. So, it is not *prima facie* explicit as to whether, how and to what extent Hinduism as a religious denomination got influenced by Vedānta.

This book is a print version of the research project completed during my tenure as senior research fellow of the Indian Council of Philosophical Research, New Delhi. I place on record my onerous gratitude to Prof. Mrinal Miri, Chairman, ICPR and his team for extending support, without which, perhaps, this book would not have seen the light of the day. I am greatly indebted to the faculty of the Centre of Advanced Study in Philosophy, Utkal University, for their constructive suggestions and moral support from time to time. I fandly remember the loving help of Dr Aditya Kumar Mohanty during the preparation of the project and its publication. Sri Radhashyam Mishra, Department of Philosophy, Utkal University, deserves special thanks for extending the meticulous secretarial assistance. My heart-felt thanks are due to D.K. Printworld, for undertaking the publication of the book.

Tapti Maitra

Contents

Preamble

THIS project begins with the presentation of a question, what is metaphysics? Obviously this question leads one to expect a discussion about metaphysics. Such is not my intention. Instead, I intend to discuss a definite metaphysical problem leading us straight to define the distinctive features of metaphysics and then, to its development to a new direction which ends with its answer to the question, what distinguishes metaphysics from the rest of philosophy. To be precise, my endeavour is to concentrate on the nature of a metaphysical inquiry.

Metaphysics is grounded in the nature of human mind or thinking. Reason is the unique possession of human species. Reason becomes functional in different forms in different modes of human pursuit. One of the distinct functions of reason consists in taking mind to a secondary awareness which enables it to subject the first order awareness to critical scrutiny. In other words, reason has an inherent property of self-transcendence. Metaphysics testifies to the flight of human reason, to scale different layers of transcendence to get at the ultimate nature of reality, the knowledge of which renders the rest of reality intelligible. Metaphysical quest is indicative of man's inherent and perpetual urge to get at the very core or essence of reality which termed as "being" (*sat*). Given the world of the phenomenal or relativity, any attempt on the part of mind to have conclusive understanding of it, takes beyond the phenomenal and invoke the noumenal. Metaphysical probe begins with the sense of awe and wonder expressing itself in the persistent effort to find the absolute behind the relative, and noumena behind the phenomena. Though the nature of metaphysical reflection differs, the underlying motivation and structure of metaphysical reflection remain the same. Since metaphysics is bound up with the basics of human mind, the choice is not between metaphysics or no-metaphysics, but between one and another. Metaphysical enquiry stands fundamentally distinct from an empirical enquiry in so far as the latter undertakes investigation into the nature of a particular, whereas the former seeks to unveil and understand the nature of the universal or the being which remains as the universal presence in and through the particulars which constitute the domain of the phenomenal.

Let us discuss the implication of the question, "what is metaphysics?", in a customary manner. The meaning of the term has changed from century to century and philosopher to philosopher. It has been held in the high esteem within the philosophical community. But to the popular mind, the subject matter is quite abstract and abstruse; the prefix "meta" was employed to refer to those things which are beyond "physics" like god and soul. There was also a division of subject matter of speculative philosophy into general metaphysics (ontology) and special metaphysics composed of natural theology. However, metaphysics in its widest sense is concerned with both the nature and structure of reality.

Metaphysics like any other philosophical inquiry, in general, has lately undergone radical revision. Functions, purposes and mannerism have been perceptibly redesigned. Contemporary metaphysics is complicated and thus there is the problem of identification. So we are forced to ask what is its nature? To understand a metaphysical scheme, we have to return to bring the relation between tradition and contemporary scene. We must understand that traditional is an endowment to the present moment by the past; tradition allows the heritage of the past experiences to develop into present experiences. This is as true in metaphysics, as it is in art and literature.

Historically speaking, the term "metaphysics" was first coined by the librarian at Alexandria while classifying and editing the works of Aristotle. It is said that the librarian was very much disturbed and disgusted with classifying a particular work of Aristotle. So out of despair, he threw the book and the book fell after the book on physics. The matter was accidental, but the librarian got the clue and termed the book as "metaphysics"; curiously enough, this historical accident explains the contents of the book. This work designated the treatise of Aristotle as well as extended to designate any philosophical work of Aristotle. For Aristotle, metaphysics is the science which studies "Being *qua* Being" and "primary being". It arises from *wonder* and *search* for the first principles and ultimate causes of everything; that which is primary is substance. At the same time, for Aristotle, metaphysics studies the basic categories in terms of which we think about the world. Seen in this light, pre-Socratic philosophers wanted to know the ultimate stuff of the universe.

The Aristotelian view of metaphysics continues to exert an influence till today. Many philosophers have agreed with Aristotle about the comprehensiveness and ultimate character of subject matter of metaphysics. For instance, Bradley says:

> We may agree perhaps, to understand by metaphysics, an attempt to know reality as against mere appearance, or the study of the first principles, or the ultimate truths, or again the effort to comprehend the universe, not simply piecemeal or by fragments, but somehow as a whole.

Both Plato and Aristotle believed that metaphysical search begins out of man's natural capacity and desire to think about himself and the world he lives in. Aristotle observed that it is owing to wonder that man began to philosophize; philosophic wonder could be called intellectual or spiritual posture. Plato also draws a self-protrait of a philosopher as a great intellectual power with quick apprehension and eager to learn the truths of the world-process. Besides, in Epistle VII, Plato gives a straightforward account of certain basic truths of metaphysics and his account of the matter throws light upon the spiritual integrity, which he considered basic to the practice of metaphysics. Memory and intelligence are insufficient to philosophizing; a nobility of soul and inner reverence for reality are moral requirements for a metaphysician; he must have dedication, loyalty and sincerity; he cannot falsely play with truth; one cannot pretend to have said the final word on it.

Two elements, consequently, seem to emerge from this picture of metaphysics: there is wonder and there is mystery; so long as there is wonder, there is metaphysics because of metaphysics. Moreover, Plato and Aristotle, diverted attention to the internal world. Accordingly, the questions of rights, liberty, justice, individuality, etc. were taken up. But metaphysical moorings were not given up. This line of thought continued to Descartes, Spinoza, Leibnitz, Kant and Hegel.

At this point, it seems logical to ask for motivation, we want to account for reasons of metaphysical pursuit and to find out what really explains the metaphysical *search*. If the answer is *wonder*, then another question: "Why wonder?" Is it natural for man to wonder? Perhaps we can enlighten this problem by putting our question to some modern thinkers view: say, Kant, Hegel, Schopenhauer and Heidegger. Kant believed that *wonder* that prompted the desire for metaphysics could be accounted for by the way the mind is constructed; the human mind, he said, is impelled to "categorize" experience. Hence, given the nature of mind, metaphysics is inevitable, even when it is bad metaphysics. "That mind will never give up metaphysics", he wrote at the end of *Prolegomena to Any Future Metaphysics*. Metaphysics is born not out of some abstract wonder but out of the "natural and unavoidable dialectic of pure reason", which superimposes metaphysical categories we make. Kant framed his conclusion about metaphysics on the basis of epistemological analysis of the different kind of statements we make. The conclusion drawn is that, synthetic a priori proposition, in philosophical knowledge, constitutes the essential subject of metaphysics. Thus Kant holds that man has a natural inclination for metaphysics, because metaphysical categories are constitutive of mind. He argues that metaphysics does not talk of transcendental reality and can hardly be called a science. What it is concerned with is, simply a way of knowing "understanding" itself. Kant adds that in metaphysics man is uncovering the mysteries of his own mind, not the mystery of universe. If metaphysics could achieve scientifically, the knowledge of *inner-reality*, the *thing-in-itself*, it would be a *transcendent science*, and it would surpass empirical experience and arrive at a *supra-empirical* knowledge.

According to Kant, the essence of things, what he called *noumena*, is incomprehensible by definition, metaphysics knows only its categories; and those categories are applied to phenomenal experience in order to make the world intelligible. Metaphysics is occupied only with reason, not with reality. Kant provided metaphysical justification of distinction of phenomena and noumena. Religion belongs to the domain of noumenon and science belongs to the domain of phenomena. Thus the question of faith and reason brought to an end to the conflict between science and religion. Now, we can mark an important point; with the rationalist approach to philosophy culminating in the system of Leibnitz, metaphysics lost its empirical origin; it was concerned with "pure reason", proceeding deductively from certain clear and distinct ideas; this was the tradition of Kant and in his *Critique of Pure Reason*, he launched on rationalist metaphysics. Consequently, metaphysics for Kant, becomes not an analysis of being, or reality as such, but an analysis of pure reason; this view he restates in his *Prolegomena to Any Future Metaphysics.*

Hegel, the classical idealist of Kantian tradition, converted the dichotomy between an analysis of reality as such and an analysis of pure reason, to a new direction; and this distinction was overcome by the claim that real is rational and rational is real. Hegel introduced dynamism into the categories of thought through the method of dialectic, a distinction between being, non-being and becoming. The universe is an all-encompassing whole. Hegelian dialectic inspired Marx and many social thinkers. Hegel's thought was so inspiring that soon many Hegelians came into being. He inspired Existentialism and Phenomenology; Hegelianism migrated into Great Britain. T.H. Green and F.H. Bradley modified Hegelianism and created their metaphysics. Besides, more direct influence on twentieth century was exerted by Hegel.

Hegel's theory of "absolute idealism" or "objective idealism" proclaims that all reality is a rational system expressed by mind or spirit and everything is a part of a single reality, called "absolute mind". Hegel also shares with contemporary thought, when he says that our thought and language give rise to philosophical puzzles and contradictions. Wittgenstein also speaks in similar tone, "philosophy is the battle against bewitchment of our understanding through the instrument of speech". J.N. Findlay, in his monumental work, *Hegel: A Re-examination,* not only re-interpreted Hegel, but tried to show many of ideas of Wittgenstein were anticipated by Hegel.

Now, we go a step further, in which Schopenhauer may help to answer our metaphysical inquiry. Perhaps he tried to find out what was left "unsaid". Leaving Kant's categories aside, Schopenhauer observes that, as man confronts world of experience, he is overwhelmed by a unique kind of wonder, which is the knowledge of his own contingency; man is haunted by imaginative and meditative melancholy, which pushes him beyond mere appearance or phenomenon into the noumenal reality, i.e. metaphysics. Metaphysics, he concluded, is not an abstract play around the structure of knowledge. Metaphysics begins in man and in his situation.

Here, we should refer to Martin Heidegger's view. He apprehends metaphysics to be engendered by a unique kind of self-knowledge, which culminates in the recognition of insufficiency; without the sense of insufficiency, man cannot have contact with metaphysics. *Dasein* (which is the presupposition of disclosure of being) exposes human life with its experiences of dread and insecurity. Man is drawn to a recognition of self-being, which is frightening. He asks metaphysical questions and he finds himself unable to explain his own existence.

To assess the features of metaphysical account offered by philosophers, we have to admit that Kant offered plausible explanation of metaphysical thought. According to him, metaphysics is something indigenous to human mind, and the way it sees thing. We also realize at this point that we have come full circle to the view of Plato on metaphysical wonder. Plato says that man is drawn by natural desire of wonder about things, because Eros, the God of desire causes man to seek higher values in experience.

Finally, we have to turn our attention to one remaining question: why does man believe in the metaphysical search? We could say that metaphysics is believable because it is self-justifying and carries its own credentials. Aristotle believed that metaphysics is the highest science, because it governs all sciences. Metaphysics proceeds by searching for the ultimate limiting notions or causes, of being as beings. Metaphysics addresses itself to an explanation of all inferior sciences, and in so doing, indicates its proper right to do so. Also, St. Thomas substantially accepted Aristotle's analysis of knowledge-structure, though he placed theology above metaphysics. But he asserted that metaphysics is the highest form of knowledge and metaphysics as the most intelligible, it cannot call upon any other knowledge to justify it because such knowledge would have to be more intelligible; and by definition, no other knowledge is more intelligible; metaphysics accounts for its own existence by its own intelligibility. Bradley also tells us, logic indicates that any attempt to disbelieve metaphysics turns itself into a metaphysical belief. If anyone denies metaphysics, "he must frame his denial in a proposition that claims to pronounce upon the character of knowledge; in turn, it requires antecedent knowledge of what knowledge is; and this is precisely the metaphysical inquiry". Here we have to take note of a philosopher of twentieth century, A.N. Whitehead, who enlightened the idea of speculative philosophy as the endeavour to frame a coherent, logical and necessary system of general ideas in terms of which every element of experience can be interpreted. He has thus both a rational and empirical side; his starting point is immediate experience, which thought has to elucidate.

From our general summary survey, a general picture emerges that metaphysics is taken by many as the heart of philosophy; also it has not been without critics; the major attack of "logical positivism" was severe. In the beginning of twentieth century, the logical positivist vehemently criticized Hegel and Hegelianism. Metaphysics is non-sense, was their slogan. Consequently, Hegelianism was thrown overboard. The Positivists tried to justify that metaphysics is "other-worldly", imaginative unfounded speculation or utterly meaningless. To some extent, they tried to reformulate and reorganize the basic metaphysical problems, still there are challenges to face them, which is not our present concern.

Similar type of movement and conceptual turmoil have taken place in India. The Cārvākas and the Buddhists revolted against metaphysical system-building. The Buddhists propounded anti-essentialism no-substance view of reality. There is no metaphysical concept of essence. They offered causal explanation for world-process, i.e. the theory of "dependent origination". According to this theory, everything is causally linked up; there is no question of absolute beginning or absolute end; no elements of supernaturalism or creationism augment their doctrine of reality; intellectualism was replaced by compassion (*mahākaruṇā*). *Nirvāṇa* (liberation) can be attained only when one realizes the impermanence of soul (*anātmā*) and this realization is called *mahāprajñā*. The other school, Cārvāka also did not entertain metaphysical theory. They have advocated the theory of "materialism"; this theory explains how matter and material laws work out philosophical question of creation. Contemporary thinker, late Prof. G. Misra interpreted Śaṅkara's Vedānta and stated that Śaṅkara was not interested in building metaphysical system. Śaṅkara was interested in the analysis of meaning and concepts. On the other hand, G.R. Malkani and many contemporary Indian thinkers have tried to defend Advaita metaphysics in their own way.

So long we have spoken of the characteristic features of metaphysics through the illustration of different types of metaphysical models. After looking briefly at some historical position of the nature of metaphysics, we will conclude with a plausible metaphysical view. In twentieth century, the publication of *Philosophical Investigation* marks a significant turn in the mode of philosophical thinking. The notion of alternative discourses with respective logical rules of their own made room for metaphysics as a form of intelligible discourse. On the one hand, it brought into focus the inherent inadequacy of the Positivist's theory of meaning and made room for multiplicity of language games, on the other. Perhaps, taking the implicit clue from Wittgensteinian vision, Strawson sought to demonstrate metaphysics as a necessary and significant philosophical exercise by drawing the distinction between "descriptive metaphysics" and "revisionary metaphysics". Unlike a scientist, who is concerned with explanation of a particular facet of reality, a metaphysician seeks to offer explanation of reality as a whole. Besides, a scientist offers causal explanation of a particular, whereas a metaphysician is one who attempts to get hold of the most basic or seminal concepts by which reality in its entirety can be explained. In Sāṁkhya metaphysics, the world with its manifold particulars is explained in terms of two basic or primitive concepts *puruṣa* and *prakṛti*. Similarly, in the metaphysics of Descartes, the world is sought to be explained by means of body and mind. These can be taken as paradigm instances of descriptive metaphysics. Given the attempts of the descriptive metaphysicians to identify and lay bare the logic of fundamental concepts, there are significant attempts to provide alternative conceptual proposals to revise the existing attempts of the descriptive metaphysics. For example, Śaṅkara directs his polemics to show the inadequacy and anomalies in the dualistic and pluralistic metaphysics, in order to make a case for monistic metaphysics, whereby reality is sought to be explained by a singular concept, *Brahman*. Similarly, Spinoza pleads in favour of monism by showing the inherent anomalies in Cartesian dualism. Thus the metaphysics of Śaṅkara and Spinoza can be taken as immaculate examples of "revisionary metaphysics". Needless to say that irrespective of the form in which metaphysical reflections are cast or re-cast, metaphysics represents the characteristic temper of human mind to find a rational and conclusive explanation of the reality as a whole and its essence, Being.

1

Formulation of Advaitism — Śaṅkara

PHILOSOPHY in ancient India was conceived to be a holistic process; it was not split up into branches. However, preoccupation with the nature, validity and avenues of knowledge is one of the characteristics and conspicuous features of Indian philosophical system; metaphysicians feel more intrigued by the problem of knowledge, which is closely associated with self (*ātman*). Śaṅkara's philosophical programme also begins with the theory of knowledge and completes with the resultant idea of self, derived from the analysis of knowing or judging. In Śaṅkara's philosophical account, it is impossible to separate epistemology from ontology because the first principle of Advaita system is conceived to be of the nature of knowledge, such as, *brahma-jñāna* or *ātma-jñāna*. And moreover, in metaphysical formulation, Śaṅkara deals with the epistemological system under three forms: *Pramāṇa*s, ontological analysis of knowledge and determination of criterion of truth; he is solely concerned with the analysis of knowledge, nature of consciousness and the relation between subject and object in cognition. Finally, he holds that valid knowledge or truth is pure consciousness or bare awareness and definition of *Brahman/ātman* signifies pure consciousness such as *sat–cit–ānanda* or *satyam, jñānam* and *anantam*. Śaṅkara has frequently used these definitions to articulate his system of Advaitism. He illustrates these three components as the constitutive of the idea of *Brahman* and explains the nature of the ultimate concept as indeterminable, unqualified, though not indefinable; Śaṅkara refers to these defining characteristics in the sense of truth or real (*satyam*), in the sense of knowledge or consciousness (*jñānam* or *cit*) and infinite or bliss used for (*anantam* or *ānanda*).

With this prefatory observation, I shall proceed to lay out Śaṅkara's formulation of Advaita doctrine before entering into the discussion of contemporary reviews on Śaṅkara's interpretation of Advaitavāda. As we know, there are different types of reviews on Śaṅkara's interpretation of Advaita Vedānta. I will discuss only Śaṅkara's philosophical programme propounded in *adhyāsa bhāṣya*, the introduction to *Brahma-Sūtra*. Śaṅkara has set his metaphysical model on the basis of analysis of knowledge to the full extent — beginning from factual knowledge (*vyāvahārika jñāna*) to the highest form of philosophical knowledge (*pāramārthika jñāna*), where the idea of *brahma-jñāna* lies embedded. These two levels of knowledge clearly indicate the transition from Advaita epistemology to Advaita metaphysics. In the process, Śaṅkara has adopted a subtle logical method to determine the validity in the gradation of knowledge, that is, from empirical to the supreme idea of philosophical knowledge. Subsequently, the empirical knowledge has been considered to be erroneous after logical scrutiny and all sorts of factual knowledge have been declared as wrong knowledge (*adhyāsa*). Consequently, the epistemic term *adhyāsa* has been substituted for all propositional forms of knowledge, because all judgemental knowledge expressed in propositional form violates logical condition of the principle of predication. Hence, I intend to illustrate the doctrine of *adhyāsa* as laid down in *adhyāsa bhāṣya*.

The doctrine of *adhyāsa* is a logical doctrine, according to which all concepts have been reviewed and reordered. The review or reordering is not a psychological operation but a logical operation. This logical doctrine has been propounded in *adhyāsa bhāṣya* and Śaṅkara establishes a criterion that, what is incorrigible, indubitable and uncontradictable, is real (*satya*). Śaṅkara and his followers have used the concept of *adhyāsa* as a logical tool for the analysis of judgement and proposition. So, I shall elucidate the function of two fundamental concepts of proposition, subject and predicate.

Analysis of Propositional Form: Subject and Predicate

Śaṅkara begins the discussion on the propositional form by pointing out that subject and predicate are two different types of concept and they are opposed to each other like light and darkness. These two contradictory ideas cannot be conjoined because this violates the principles of logic. One idea cannot be applied to its opposite sphere because the subject is real and the predicate unreal. Any attempt to put these two ideas together leads to wrong consequences (*mithyā-jñāna*). Śaṅkara ascertains that subject and predicate belong to two different categories and make a logical distinction of subject and predicate — *ātman* and *anātman*. According to him, there is a fundamental antithesis between them because *ātman* is real (*satya*) and *anātman* is unreal (*asat* or *anṛta*); they are two different and distinct ideas. On this ground Śaṅkara maintains the logical and categorical distinction between subject and predicate; they are not of the same type and belong to two different logical classes, *viṣayī* and *viṣaya*. Śaṅkara also points out that subject and predicate function in different manners. The subject forms the referring part, it is an individually identifying expression; the predicate forms the descriptive part of assertion, it is a character-ascribing expression; this distinction implies a distinction of characterization and identification. Śaṅkara also argues that subject and predicate cannot be related because they are mutually exclusive ideas; their nature is of absolute contrast; they belong to different categories with distinct and opposite characteristics. As they are two distinct ideas, they cannot be held together and their combination in propositional form is logically wrong. But we are always involved in the logical error of identifying two different concepts in propositional symbolism, and, therefore, all knowledge which is propositional is logically false. And *adhyāsa* means this wrong identification of two contrasting ideas, that is, identification of real with unreal and existent with non-existent. This combination of two opposite elements violates the logical principle. But we commit this mistake and thereby are involved in perpetual logical error, i.e. *adhyāsa*. Śaṅkara's statements, *satyānr̥te mithunīkr̥tyā* and *mithyeti bhābitum yuktam,* signify that the coupling of subject and predicate in propositional context is not logically correct. Neither the predicate (*viṣaya*) nor its properties (*dharma*) can be ascribed to the subject and vice versa. From the very beginning Śaṅkara warns us that the coupling of subject and predicate (*satya* and *anr̥ta*) in propositional symbolism is logically wrong (*mithyā*), and finally he sums up that every judgement is corrigible in respect of the predicate, on account of the corrigibility of the predicate.

Moreover, Śaṅkara has some other ground for saying that every judgement is corrigible in respect of the predicate part, because in judging something there is the possibility of misjudging. But the subject is never infected by this possibility. In this respect the subject is real (*satya*) and the predicate is unreal (*anr̥ta*). Besides, the predicate expression cannot present a fact in its own right and to that extent it is incomplete. But the subject expression such as "this", or "that", or "I" presents a fact in its own right and is therefore self-complete. A predicate cannot be used independently and requires a substratum (*adhiṣṭhāna*). Predicates are ideas (*kalpanā*s) and they must be applied to a subject; there is incompleteness of meaning in all predicates, and they have to depend upon the subject for a meaningful expression. The same analysis of the nature of predicate has been expressed in modern terminology and some contemporary logicians say that predicates or universals (sortal type or characterizing type) are ideas, whereas particulars or subjects are things or facts. The particular is invariable; the subject "I" remains the same and various predicates are ascribed to it. This shows that variability is an essential characteristic of predicates. But these two elements are necessary for a complete thought, though predicates are "unsaturated" and subjects are "saturated". Subjects and predicates are two moments of cognition; they have different status; still their coupling has been admitted in a factual statement. According to Śaṅkara, in spite of the differences of subject and predicate, they are unified in factual level till we develop the critical faculty of discrimination of true knowledge of *Brahman* or *ātman*. In *adhyāsa bhāṣya* he has also interpreted the concept of *ātman* as *asmad*, designated by the word "I" and *asmad* becomes related with *anātman* (*yuṣmad*) by way of predication in propositional knowledge without being affected by such a contingent relation. To speak in contemporary idioms, we are never mistaken about the particulars but there is always a possibility of mistake in respect of universals, e.g. red, blue, table, tree and pot. Since the predicate has a general sense, it can be applied to any subject.

So all these arguments are good enough to show that in *adhyāsa bhāṣya*, Śaṅkara intends to talk about the type difference of two concepts. He is only concerned with the logicality that can be challenged of propositional knowledge and he wants to give a logical account for this. He has pointed out the difference (*virodha*) of two elements in every proposition of which one is real and the other unreal, and cannot therefore be linked up. But all propositions are due to the coupling of logical predicate to a logical subject. Every proposition is, for the Advaitins, subject–predicate type, and every judgement contains two elements of opposite character. Śaṅkara traces out this traditional association between subject and predicate to wrong identification of two concepts and describes it as linguistic convention (*naisargika-adhyāsa*) and unification of these two concepts is possible only in factual statement. False cognition is beginningless (*anādi*) and wrong knowledge arises because of our ignorance (*avidyā*) about the fundamental difference between these two logical categories, subject and predicate, the real and unreal. This ignorance is an inherent characteristic of human nature; our conviction is so much deep-rooted that we are unable to discriminate the real from the unreal. Hence we cannot determine the real nature of thing (*vastu svarūpa avadhāna*), which Śaṅkara considers to be the fundamental characteristic of knowledge (*vidyā*).

Principle of Predication

So far we have discussed Śaṅkara's description of the manner of occurrence of subject and predicate in propositional knowledge. When asked to state his doctrine of predication involving the corrigibility of judgement on account of predicate, he answers in three statements:

1. Error may be due to application of concepts to new cases, because application of concepts is aided by memory.
2. Error may occur in such cases when a thing is cognized in a form which is the form of another thing, or a thing is described by the attribute of another.
3. Error may be due to the identification of something which is not that (erroneous identification of subject with predicate).

This is how Śaṅkara illustrates the definition of *adhyāsa*. We shall analyse these statements separately to clear all sorts of confusion and to show that they are not psychological statements, but are, on the contrary, three ways of predication.

FIRST STATEMENT

smṛtirūpaḥ-paratra-pūrvadṛṣṭa-avabhāsaḥ[1]

This statement is the most significant of the three; it is the precise definition of the concept of *adhyāsa*. If we analyse this statement we will find that it signifies logical character and does not represent any psychological fact. The word *pūrvadṛṣṭa* does not mean mental image as usually supposed by the interpreters of Advaita philosophy. So also, the word *smṛtirūpaḥ* does not indicate any psychological process of memory; it signifies that whenever we apply a concept, we assume that the present case is similar to the other members of the class signified by the concept. Similarly, the word *avabhāsa* need not be understood as a reflection or image of the object of knowledge; it implies that all predicates can be replaced or changed and they have no fixed application to particular cases like proper names. The concept of *avabhāsa* is not a psychological process of illusion. When a general idea is subsequently changed into another, for example, the idea of silver is changed into that of shell, the process is called *avabhāsa*. As a philosophical logician, Śaṅkara is concerned with the general principle of predication and does not wish to point out any mistake in the perceptual process of seeing one moon as double, or rope as snake. Predication is not a psychological activity. In the act of judging, we apply concepts, and in order to apply concepts we must know how it has been used in previous cases (*pūrvadṛṣṭa*). On the basis of acquired knowledge of that concept, we apply it to new cases (*paratra*s) present before us. Such an application may be wrong because in applying a concept we rely upon memory which is fallible. So it follows inevitably that *adhyāsa* is judgement involving memory but not an exact case of memory (*smṛtirūpa*). Again,

---

1 Śaṅkara, *Adhyāsabhāṣya* (tr. Pandit Kalivara Veadanta Vagish — *Vedānta Darśanam*, pub. by Khirod Chandra Majumdar, Calcutta), 1970, part I, p. 7.

this statement forms a general principle of predication for propositional knowledge or any type of meaningful expression in linguistic structure. Usually we make such statements as "this is a table", "that is a cow", "that is a rope", "this is a pot", etc. Each of them involves two elements: one is perceptual element, viz. "this", "that", as something present before us, and the other is memory element, viz. our assertion of table, cow, etc. In apprehending "this" as table or cow, memory is involved; in describing a thing we depend on our memory. As predication involves memory, it is not logically certain; all predication involves an actuality as well as the logical possibility of falsehood.

Thus, in the above consideration, we see that Śaṅkara derives a general theory of error from factual cases of error. In describing a thing or asserting something, the predicate part carries a possibility of misdescription. All statements are open to the possibility of logical error due to the open texture of predicate. Falsity lies in our way of predication. But the subject of all judgements or the referring part remains unaffected and it is incorrigible. Corrigibility of knowledge comes in predicate. "This" as a subject (*viṣayī*) remains unchanged, whereas the predicate (*viṣaya*) varies on different occasions for meaningful expression. But my judging some thing as "this" or "that" does not change. "This", "that", and "I" are pure referents and the referring part does not describe anything; so there is no possibility of mistake in them. They are simply demonstrative components. Within knowledge, referring part cannot be suspected, but my description is doubtful. The subject expression, "this", can never be misapplied, but the predicate expression, "is a cow", may be misapplied. That is why Śaṅkara denounces the descriptive part of expression as corrigible (*prapañca*) and regards the validity of the referring part, "I", or "this", or "that". They are the logical subjects, and predicates are always attached to the subject for a meaningful expression.

SECOND STATEMENT

anyasya anyadharma avabhāṣatām[2]

The second statement may be considered a variation of the first statement. This statement implies that when a thing is described by the quality (*dharma*) of another thing, or a thing is cognized in the form of another thing, such description or cognition, also, is a case of wrong knowledge, i.e. *adhyāsa*. Śaṅkara specifically mentions that any quality of the predicate cannot be applied to the subject, i.e. *ātman*, because predicates belong to a different class. This statement indicates that all judgements are wrong, because application of descriptive words carries the possibility of mistakes. Whenever there is a case of judging something, there is also the possibility of misjudging it. For the clarification of this logical point, Śaṅkara refers to the factual error of snake in rope or silver in shell. People do commit such factual mistakes, and if some judgements are wrong, then other judgements cannot claim absolute certainty. So we should not wonder when Śaṅkara denounces all judgements as false because of the factual mistake involved in some judgements. All predicates are ideas (*kalpanā*s) and not facts; due to their free-floating nature, they may be applied rightly or wrongly. Hence Śaṅkara characteristically mentions that "this" and "I" (*idam* and *aham*) are logical subjects and their use in language is different; there is definite linguistic rule for their use while predicates do not have such fixed rule for their use in language. Besides, the particulars have stability in expression, for example, "I" cannot be used in asserting silver. I cannot say "I am silver", but I shall have to say "this is silver". It is clear that the linguistic usage of subject and predicate is different. So we should not combine these two ideas, nor should we ascribe the characteristic (*dharma*) of one to the other, since they cannot be placed under the same class.

---

[2] Śaṅkara, *Adhyāsabhāṣya*, p. 12.

THIRD STATEMENT

atasmin tadbuddhi[3]

The third statement, again, follows from the second, and in this statement, Śaṅkara finally sums up his doctrine of *adhyāsa*. This statement implies that the identification of subject (*ātman*) with predicate (*anātman*) is erroneous. In knowledge, we identify the subject with the predicate by combining them into propositional form. This is a wrong identification resulting in wrong knowledge and, therefore, a case of *adhyāsa*. There are several ways in which misidentification of subject with predicate can occur, and Śaṅkara illustrates this with certain factual cases. Sometimes we ascribe to the subject (*ātman*) some external qualities, when we say my son, my property, my house, etc. — these are physical predicates. We also ascribe to *ātman* the attributes of body, senses, etc., such as "I am fat" and "I am blind". Again, we identify *ātman* with *antaḥkaraṇa* and ascribe mental predicates to the subject, e.g. "I wish", "I determine", "I doubt" and "I consider". These are the different ways in which the subject is characterized by different predicates leading to a wrong identification. These statements clearly indicate that, as all these characterizations are false, thus so, all predications to the subject are also false. We cannot ascribe to *ātman* any quality, physical or mental; *ātman* cannot be described in any language. By attributing characteristics, it brings in plurality into that which is *adyaya*, *asaṅga* and *nirguṇa*. Śaṅkara describes such wrong identification as *mithyā-pratyaya*, that is, misuse of concepts, which is found to be beginningless and endless in the natural order of language (*anādi* and *ananta*). So, predicates or universals, sortal type or characterizing type, may be ascribed to the logical subject, and this will not affect the concept of *ātman* as *nirguṇa* (without any attribute). The words like "I", "this" and "that" stand for the subject of

3 Śaṅkara, *Adhyāsabhāṣya*, p. 27.

knowledge, and therefore, they are referents. The individual subject (*pradeśika-ātman*) is the knower (*pramātā*), and this knower is a logical requirement for factual knowledge; the concept of "I" is used as *aham-pratyaya-viṣayī* in Śaṅkara's epistemology. The expressions — *pradeśika-ātman*, *pramātā* and *aham-pratyaya-viṣayī* — are used as subjects of cognitive statements, because there must be a referent; a statement without reference is unthinkable. Śaṅkara has used these expressions whenever he has talked of *vyāvahārika jñāna* (empirical knowledge). But eminent scholars have understood them as the limited forms of *ātman*. Thus we may conclude that the doctrine of *adhyāsa* signifies the logical thesis that the referring part of a judgement is consistent, whereas the descriptive part of it is inconsistent, a wrong concept.

Resultant Concept

From this part of discussion of the doctrine of *adhyāsa* (erroneous knowledge), two things emerge clearly; the absolute certainty of the subject (*ātman*) and the falsifiability of the predicate (*anātman*); the unreality of two fundamental substances (*dvaita*) has been demonstrated by this logical doctrine. The method adopted in explaining the concept of *adhyāsa* includes only analysis of judgemental knowledge and not of any psychological act in judging or misjudging. Śaṅkara begins with the logical distinction of subject and predicate, which accounts for his broad division of real and unreal, true and false, active and passive, self-complete and incomplete, and there are several pairs, expressing these ideas such as, *sat* and *asat*, *satya* and *anṛta* and *jaḍa* and *ajaḍa*.

To sum up, Śaṅkara has criticized judgements from three angles:

1. Subject and predicate, being two different types of concept, cannot be coupled.
2. As predicate is unstable and variable, it is fraught with

the possibility of being misapplied and is, therefore, corrigible and unreal.

3. The validity of predicates is not acceptable for their corrigible nature; they are called *prapañca* (that which takes different forms). True knowledge remains unchangeable + uncontradictable and it is expressed as "bare knowledge" without a subject–predicate form. Subject ceases to be subject when all predicates are discarded; consequently, bare knowledge is left with.

Evidently, Śaṅkara in the analysis of the concept of *adhyāsa* intends to show that *ātman* (logical subject) is the fundamental concept. In illustration, Śaṅkara chooses demonstrative pronouns such as "I", "this" and "that" as suitable expressions for logical subject, because these expressions can never be mistaken. There cannot be any question regarding their certainty and he keeps them in a distinct category. The concept of "this" or "that" or "I" does not involve any descriptive element; it is a point of reference or demonstrative word. So there is no possibility of error in these expressions. These concepts can never be used misidentifyingly, and they can exist even without ascription of predicate. They have independent status and are absolutely certain, whereas predicates have no independent status; they have to be linked up with a subject. They are also found to be uncertain because they go on changing.

It appears that Śaṅkara and his contemporaries have been attracted by the idea of pure demonstrative expressions. It seems that Śaṅkara is interested only to find out such statements as would be immuned from logical doubt and accepts these basic concepts of "I" and "this" which are indubitable and not subject to further test. The pure demonstrative expressions are directly and conclusively verifiable. But this is not possible in the case of descriptive expressions. It is held that "I" and "this" are incorrigible in the sense that they cannot be doubted or denied. But maintaining absolute certainty of these concepts, which do not describe any character of experience, leaves no room for knowledge. So there is nothing for one to be certain or mistaken about. But it is true that there is no class of descriptive statements which are incorrigible. However strong the experience on the basis of which a descriptive statement is put forward, the possibility of its falsehood cannot be excluded. Complete security can be attained only by the statement like "I am" or "that is that", *aham* or *tat*, the symbolic expression used for *ātman*.

It is worth-noting that in Advaita framework there is a distinct transition from epistemology to metaphysics. As a result the demonstrative expressions, such as "I", "it", "this" and "that" cease to be mere verbal symbols referringly used, but are significant of ontological substratum. Just as the pure subject is not subjected to contingencies of sublation like the predicates, the universal substratum remains immune to any kind of contingency or change. That is why Truth comes to be defined as something which suffers no consequences (*satyam apariṇāmī*). In other words, it is not subject to the process of sublation in principle (*satyam avādhītam*). The selfsame substratum is termed as *Brahman* and *ātman* in its macrocosmic and microcosmic sense, respectively.

Ātman: Defining Characteristics

Śaṅkara tries to find out a criterion that has absolute certainty from the logical standpoint, and discards everything that is not in conformity with the logical criterion. He starts his philosophical discussion with the analysis of knowledge and proves the logical validity of the concept of subject (*ātman*). The occurrence of the concept of *ātman* in knowledge is undeniable in the sense that whenever I say something, I have to say it with reference to the subject. This "subject" has been expressed in various ways: *pramātṛcaitanya, idamabacchinna caitanya, aham pratyaya-viṣayī*, corresponding to the pronouns "this" or "that" and "it" and "I". These are fundamental concepts required for any meaningful expression. Śaṅkara analyses the concept of knowledge and finds that these terms form the basic structure of knowledge. From the epistemological analysis he proceeds to establish his conclusion regarding the ultimate reality or the concept of *ātman*, which has been expressed through the medium of the above terms.

The word *ātman* signifies the idea of pure knowledge or bare awareness (*caitanya*) or pure consciousness or *sākṣī-jñāna* (witnessing), etc., "this", "that", "it", "I" — these referring expressions have been used for the concept of *ātman* in Advaita literature. Because these referring expressions cannot be misused — their use is identical with their correct use. These pure referents convey the true meaning of the word *ātman* — the logical subject of any kind of knowledge, without any attribute. Again, the subject (*ātman*) refers to "I", or "this", or "that", which cannot be identified with any physical concept; it is a logical concept and in this sense it is trans-empirical or may be called transcendental. This idea of subject is unchangeable; this idea of *ātman* is the primitive idea or "category" of Advaita philosophy (Karl H. Potter, *Encyclopedia of Indian Philosophies*, vol. III); it cannot be shaken off like other facts. *Ātman* is the subject of every judgement, every predication; it always refers to the subject of knowledge — "I", "this" and "that". These words bear definite expression; they are essential elements of logical as well as factual discourse. These words form the substantial part of all cases of knowledge. So the true meaning of the term *ātman* implies the substantial, non-dual, identical character of the logical subject in every proposition. This concept also signifies an unchangeable principle in knowledge, a permanent concept that has been employed to distinguish between corrigible and incorrigible ideas. "This" or "I" as logical subject is a necessary presupposition for all knowledge, as every knowledge has a subject, the knower; knowledge without a knower involves contradiction; there is no knowledge without a knower. The subject is the immutable and indubitable part of knowledge, though the content is dubitable. Here Śaṅkara has rightly asserted that validity of knowledge becomes intelligible only on the acceptance of a knower which signifies the logical subject. The limit of knowledge is the subject. The subject or the *Ātman* is the transcendental principle of all knowledge, but it should not be taken as a transcendental entity; it is required for every occasion of knowledge but does not constitute any part of descriptive knowledge. Any piece of knowledge can be doubted, whereas the principle underlying the concept of knowledge is indisputable. It is like the principle of the game in which knowledge of a particular game is acquired but forms no part of the game itself. In the same way, the concept of *ātman* forms the boundary of knowledge but does not fall within the boundary. Further, Śaṅkara has acknowledged that any corporeal or non-corporeal qualities may be attributed to "I", e.g. "I am fat", "I am lame" and "I am happy". In all these instances, "I" has been attributed by the qualities of body, sense, mind, but "I" does not change due to these various attributions and remains as invariable eternal principle of knowledge. Thus the notion of *ātman* or "I" is indubitable and irrefutable.

The Advaitins describe *ātman* as pure consciousness (*caitanya*), non-dual (*advaita*) and qualityless (*nirguṇa*). But consciousness is not an attribute of *ātman*; it is the defining characteristic of *ātman*. *Ātman* is pure consciousness, i.e. bare awareness, and not something having the attribute of consciousness; consciousness is not possessed by *ātman* in the same way as a cow is possessed by Caitra or Maitra. *Ātman* should not be taken as a substantive and consciousness as an attributive. This idea of pure consciousness implies bare knowledge without any distinction of subject and predicate. *Ātman* is known as "just something being there" (*tat*), the existence of something as "this" (*idam*).

Different idioms have been introduced to signify the meaning of *ātman* and *Brahman*, such as *kūṭastha–nitya*, *pratyagātman* and *sat–cit–ānanda*. It is also noticeable that none of these ideas means any hidden concept or some entity beyond this empirical world. By analysing these terms it will be found that they are not the denizens of a transcendental world parallel to this world, but all of them signify pure logical concepts. As an illustrative instance, I shall try to explain the meaning of the expression, *sat–cit–ānanda*.

Sat–Cit–Ānanda

The later Advaitins have combined the three distinct ideas, viz. *sat*, *cit* and *ānanda* into one composite idea, a triad. Śaṅkara always treated them separately while interpreting the *Brama-Sūtra-Bhāṣya*. However, this term signifies a self-complete idea of *Brahman*, which exists by itself, occurs by itself and, can, therefore, be metaphorically called self-enjoying, "bliss of Brahman lies in its being full (*pūrṇa*)" (Potter, p. 76). *Ātman* or *Brahman* means consciousness (*cit*) and not that a substance possessing a quality called consciousness; it is mere awareness of something; *ātman*/*Brahman* means existence (*sat*) — pure being. Again, *ātman* cannot be defined as mere consciousness or mere existence; these two concepts — existence and consciousness — have been combined to constitute the meaning of the concept of *ātman* and *Brahman*. Consciousness and existence are covered under one concept, and they are not two attributes; *sat* and *cit*, existence and consciousness are inseparable ideas composing the one unitary idea of *Brahman*.

Sat–cit–ānanda is the most significant concept of the Advaita philosophy. This is the genuine expression conveying the real character of the logical concept, *ātman* or *Brahman*. Their assertion of "existence" and "consciousness" is based on the analysis of knowledge, and *ātman* as the incorrigible principle of knowledge is philosophically illuminating. Everything may be denied but the very denial presupposes consciousness (*caitanya*) or mere awareness of "something" (*sat*). So also, pointing out the contingent character of the object of knowledge, the Advaitins have arrived at the conclusion that "pure-existence" as such cannot be denied. The existence of a particular object can be denied, and this is usually found in our ordinary experience when we are unable to determine the nature of the object of knowledge. But that "something" ("that" or *tat*) is there which is characterized by me as x or y cannot be denied. My characterization of the thing may be false, but that there is "something" existent which is pointed out by me cannot be false. If we analyse perceptual knowledge such as "this is a table", we will see that our knowledge of the object may not be valid but the subject part cannot be false; the knowledge of table may be falsified but the subject, "this", is unmistakable.

Further, existence without consciousness involves contradiction. When I assert the existence of something, I am aware of it; existence and consciousness go together, I know *P*, my assertion of *P* may be false, but that I know something cannot be false. In every act of knowledge, both consciousness and existence must be there. Consciousness (*caitanya*) has a wider meaning comprehending the idea of subject, the idea of object and the idea of the method of knowing. No knowledge is devoid of consciousness or awareness of something. Thus the concepts of *sat* and *cit* together make an incorrigible principle of knowledge which is the conclusion of Advaita philosophy. *Ātman* or *Brahman* may be variously attributed, but all attributions have been turned down as false on logical ground. *Ātman* and *Brahman* can be expressed only as "that is that" (*tat-tvam-asi*). According to Advaita Vedānta, "pure consciousness" and "pure existence" have logical certainty, and what is logically certain is real. That is why *Brahman* has been described as "*nirguṇa*", no quality should be ascribed to it. It is existence and consciousness; it is pure "this" or "that" or "I".

Identity of Ātman and Brahman

It is worth emphasizing that the nature of attribution or analysis undertaken to elucidate nature of *ātman* is also taken to be true of *Brahman*. This equivocally points to the thesis of unqualified identity of *ātman* and *Brahman*. Logical analysis of the states of the subject presupposes a unifying concept, that is, *ātman*; it is the basis of all description about the subject, but itself is indescribable. Similarly, the analysis of the objective world presupposes or leads to a unifying concept, i.e. *Brahman*. There cannot be two unifying principles. That which is indescribable is bound to be one. So, *ātman* is *Brahman*, and *Brahman* is *ātman*. If one begins with individual consciousness or *jīva*, one arrives at *ātman* as basis of all sorts of consciousness. If one begins from the world, one arrives at *Brahman* which is indescribable (*anirvacanīya*) in nature. This is how Śaṅkara has formulated the monistic doctrine of Advaita. Though I have characterized the Advaita concepts of *ātman* and *Brahman* as ultimate metaphysical principle and logical presupposition of all discourse and knowledge, yet the metaphysical/logical principle has played a major role in shaping up the Indian tradition, and influenced and moulded the attitude of millions in this country. Philosophy, being a foundational and fundamental discipline, has influenced the man and the society in many ways both in the West and the East; it has contributed to the society and the culture.

2

Metaphysics of Advaita Vedānta A Review — G.R. Malkani

A NUMBER of Indian professional philosophers have presented different interpretations of classical Vedānta doctrine in contemporary idioms and concepts, used in contemporary philosophical literature. G.R. Malkani is one of the luminaries of great philosophers. He had devoted his academic life to the propagation of Advaita point of view. His exposition of Advaita Vedānta has a unique philosophical orientation. In this chapter, I intend to give a brief account of Malkani's review of Advaitic ideas as reflected in his book, *Metaphysics of Advaita Vedānta*. Malkani, in the opening lines of this book, speaks about the specific character of Advaita system as the highest expression of Hindu metaphysical thinking and it propounds "purest philosophical truth. This system is clear, bold in conception and uncompromising in its logic" (Malkani's version). He further adds that the whole effort in Advaita Vedānta is to reach the knowledge of the truth which fulfils reason and, consequently, problems of thought fall away; then there is absolute certainty. Malkani intends to expound the theory of Advaita Vedānta as a living system, though ancient. His attitude is different from the traditional oriental scholars; his interpretation is solely based on the Upaniṣadic views. His presentation of Advaita thought is genuine, a free presentation of a "truth seeker" (Malkani). Moreover, his philosophical account is not infected by any type of speculative method or mysticism. He believes that mysticism has no truth value, it is an imagination. So, Malkani tries to find out a possibility with a species of direct knowledge "confirmed by reason and consolidated by will" (Malkani, p. vii). Accordingly he proceeds to elucidate the distinctive feature of Advaita Vedānta and to define the goal of the Advaitins, that is, the goal to seek the Absolute Truth; in Advaita Vedānta, desire for true knowledge finds out the way for its perfect fulfilment. With this comprehensive remarks on the outline of Advaita philosophy, Malkani attempts to lay out the central theme of Advaita, its religion and philosophy.

Advaita Theology

Malkani begins with the Advaita theory of religion as a prelude to Advaita metaphysics, since he considers that there are some Western philosophers, either rationalist or idealist, who start philosophical venture with certain strictly defined concepts, which they think, cannot be doubted and ought to be universally accepted. Out of these concepts, they develop a whole system of thought through a form of Deductive Reasoning. Malkani admits that Advaitism as a system of philosophy, also propounds a system of concepts through which we can understand and interpret fundamental concept, *Brahman* (Absolute); Advaitism also tries to present the conception of reality as a "whole intelligible in terms of certain concepts". But he points out that mere system of concepts is not enough to reach the goal of Advaita philosophical entrepreneur, i.e. proper knowledge (*pāramārthika jñāna*) (*brahma-vidyā*); as indicated in Malkani's philosophical statement: "to know the Ultimate Truth or Reality, mere concepts are not enough". So, Malkani suggests that we require a method to operate our intuitive apparatus. Since no normal agency of knowledge can lead us to the knowledge of reality, in philosophical sense, Malkani believes:

> Advaitism has a recourse to super-normal method. This is the revealed word (*śruti*). We know the ultimate metaphysical truth with the aid of certain Upaniṣadic texts. Thus Advaitism is both a philosophy and religion.[1]

Now, I shall present this new feature of Advaita Vedānta, indicating Malkani's excellence in the orientation of Advaitism as a synthesis of philosophy and religion. I shall try to explain how Malkani brought out a synthesis of philosophy and religion in Advaita Vedānta. Malkani initiates his discussion on the referred theme with a general remark that religious concept of Advaita system is a necessary factor in understanding the Advaita conception of *Brahman*, the Absolute. Malkani points out the inadequacy of our common understanding on the basis of our sensible contact with reality, because we are incapable of transcending this contact. So, our common knowledge needs a higher source of knowledge to acquire the knowledge of Reality (*tattva-jñāna*). And Malkani concedes that this higher source can be no other than the "revealed religion"; this remark implies a unique blend of philosophy and religion in Advaita Vedānta. Further, Malkani classifies the Advaita method of knowledge in two important instruments of religion — the revealed word and the tradition — both of them are required to acquire philosophical knowledge (*tattva-jñāna*). That is why Malkani describes Advaitism as a religion which seeks perfect knowledge. "It is the religion of knowledge."[2]

So, Malkani pursues to demonstrate how Advaitism generates higher kind of knowledge, since knowledge (*jñāna*) is the central theme of both Advaita philosophy and Advaita theology. Malkani has marked out the distinctive feature of Advaita theory of knowledge which is qualified as necessary

---

[1] G.R. Malkani, *Metaphysics of Advaita Vedānta*, Amalner: The Indian Institute of Philosophy, 1961, p. 3.

[2] Ibid., p. 4.

and certain from logical point of view — this type of knowledge is the content of both Advaita philosophy and religion; this kind of knowledge is not subject to cancellation (*bādha*) by any later or subsequent knowledge; this is the proper knowledge in Advaita system. Malkani describes that this type of knowledge as the knowledge of the ultimate ground of this world, the ultimate source of creation.

> This ground is necessarily invisible, super-sensible and metaphysical. It is the higher reality that underlies all things and is the truth of all things. It is called by Upaniṣads, *Brahman*.[3]

With this outline of religious and philosophical aspects of Advaitism, Malkani concentrates upon the special feature of the Advaita religion. Obviously, the sense of the expression "Advaita religion" does not function as ordinary sense of religion in our society. In religious pursuit, Advaita philosophers try to find out the root cause of ignorance, creating all sorts of social evil; in their persistent pursuit, they confirm that all sorts of human sufferings are due to ignorance of truth. Therefore, all human sufferings will come to an end by the knowledge of Truth, direct and certain; this is the supreme knowledge and the highest value (*mokṣa*), which is the ideal of all human endeavour. Malkani articulates his view in the following lines:

> It is the purest, the noblest and most satisfying. Thus philosophy becomes, in Advaitism, the highest form of religion. It gives the saving knowledge, which leads to Absolute Freedom called *mokṣa*. This conception of philosophy differs fundamentally from the generally accepted Western conception, according to which philosophy is a purely intellectual pursuit and can only satisfy a certain intellectual curiosity or a desire for the

---

[3] Malkani, op. cit., p. 4.

> unification of all knowledge. In Indian philosophy, on the other hand, value is the very breath of philosophy. And what value can be greater than Freedom or Bliss?[4]

Malkani also justifies that all the important elements of religion have been codified in Advaita thought, like, faith in the scripture, disciplineship, the goal of self-realization and all those inner qualities of moral purities which are necessary for the knowledge of the Highest Spiritual Reality. So Malkani asserts that Advaita religion is not a religion as ordinarily understood; it is the religion of Truth which supersedes all other religions. Furthermore, Malkani elaborates the characteristics of Advaitism as "great religion", because Advaita religion does not emphasize much on the various factors of embodied existence. On the other hand, Advaitism directs us to a proper recourse of release from empirical existence. He observes the contention of the Advaitins which suggests that we are by *nature* divine and nothing can change that nature as we cannot change the nature of fire to burn. Malkani also believes in Advaita theory:

> Our true self is essentially self-luminous and blissful. Only our embodiedness, which itself is a result of ignorance, has covered up this nature and made it appear different from what it really is. . . . We are thus *alienated* from our real Self through *ignorance* alone, and become subject to all the ills of the body and the mind. When knowledge arises, it puts an end to all suffering. Our release is complete and final.[5]

In the quoted lines, Malkani ascertains that true knowledge dispels our ignorance; when it is dispelled, it is dispelled for good. It cannot *recur*. Knowledge is invariably and necessarily preceded by ignorance, but ignorance is *not* preceded by knowledge. Therefore, when knowledge arises, there is

---

4 Malkani, op. cit., p. 4.

5 Ibid., p. 5.

complete and final end of ignorance, complete cessation of all ills. Thus knowledge proper or "true knowledge is a direct awareness of reality as reality is".[6] This is the genuine point of Advaita theory of knowledge. In Advaita Vedānta, there is only one valid form of knowledge, that is, the knowledge of *Brahman*, "which has the character of literal truth. To know *Brahman* is to have a life in the Truth."[7] All religions also seek this kind of life and direct us to achieve this goal by the acquisition of the knowledge of Reality. In this way, Advaitism enables us to reach the highest level of knowledge and to free us from human evils; in the process, Advaitism formulates its metaphysical doctrine following the principle of religion of knowledge.

From this brief account, it is clear that Malkani intends to present the central theme of Advaita Vedānta comprising two aspects of Advaitism, i.e. philosophy moulded with religion and the spiritual goal. It has to be noted that Advaita theory of religion has been properly characterized by Malkani as philosophy of knowledge, truth and reality, i.e. *brahma-vidyā*. Obviously, as a natural sequence, the account of Truth, Reality and Knowledge comes under the Advaita theory of religion and this kind of knowledge with absolute certainty is not ordinary commonsense knowledge; it is the highest form of knowledge which in Advaita terminology called *brahma-vidyā*. Needless to say that it is not knowledge of ordinary intellectual variety. The attainment of *brahma-vidyā* is the spiritual aspiration of all human beings. Here is the meeting point of religion with metaphysical knowledge. The ordinary mode of knowledge is not competent for such type of higher knowledge. Hence, Advaitins have prescribed certain methods to acquire *brahma-vidyā*; this method for dispelling ignorance

---

6 Malkani, op. cit., p. 6.

7 Ibid.

is called *pramāṇa*; *pramāṇa* includes common methods of knowledge along with some spiritual course, such as *vairāgya*, which means renouncement of mundane pleasure; *nityānitya vastuviveka*, which signifies ability to discriminate between real and unreal; and lastly, there must be an earnest desire for true knowledge (*mumukṣā*). All these moral and spiritual disciplines can be regulated by feeling and will. Above all, the revealed word (*śruti*) is considered as the proper method for acquiring higher knowledge or metaphysical knowledge (*brahma-vidyā*). In this context Malkani has enlightened the role and significance of the revealed word (*śruti*) as the specific method of knowledge for acquiring *brahma-vidyā*. Malkani also clarifies that this method is not a method of sensible experience, but a positive intuition of super-sensible reality; for instance, our knowledge of the self is not based on any sensible intuition. It is a sort of "mixed intuition", this type of intuition and the revealed word (*śruti*) have been recognized as a special method in Advaita epistemology; intuitive experience and the revealed word are the main recourse for the realization of Absolute Truth.

But a question may arise, whether the word is sufficient for the purpose of metaphysical knowledge. Malkani contends that word is sufficient to give direct knowledge, but it is not sufficient to remove all our doubts. Sometimes there may be a doubt about the correct interpretation of scriptural statement. This doubt can only be removed through the process of reasoning based on the rules of correct interpretations. When we have got the correct interpretation, it gives unity and significance to all scriptural statements. Malkani acknowledges:

> This is philosophy proper, where reason is used constructively for the elucidation of truth in experience. . . . The mind, though rationally convinced, is prone to waver on account of wrong habits of thought. . . . A spiritual process

> of one-pointed contemplation becomes necessary. When it reaches a high degree of steadiness and perfection, metaphysical knowledge becomes a living thing.[8]

Subsequently, Malkani refers to different processes required for metaphysical knowledge. To sum up, first, hearing the truth (*śravaṇa*), then reflection (*manana*) and finally contemplation (*nididhyāsana*), each step logically leads to the next one till our knowledge is perfected. Here, again we find a blend of knowledge and spiritual goal of religion. Finally, Malkani has noted down the characteristics of true knowledge in Advaita Vedānta; logically speaking true knowledge means necessary truth, not the resultant of sense perception; true knowledge is self-evidently true. He explains the Advaita view that "knowledge will be true only if there is some other kind of reality, which cannot fail, by its very nature, to communicate itself directly".[9] Malkani also admits that what can be truly known by us is contrast to this physical reality; it is a kind of spiritual reality and also entitled as absolute knowledge in Advaita Vedānta. Again, a spiritual reality is essentially an intelligent reality as assumed by Malkani:

> A spiritual reality is essentially an intelligent reality. A reality is intelligent when it knows. It knows whatever is given to it or presented to it. But that is only one side of its nature. Its other side is that it is not presented to another or known by another. The moment it is known by another, it becomes non-intelligent or *jaḍa*. It becomes part of nature. It ceases to be spirit. The true spirit knows, but is not known.[10]

In the above lines, Malkani clearly portrays the Advaita concept of knowledge as a spiritual intelligent concept. This notion of intelligent reality is self-revealing and self-evident. This form of intelligent reality is *absolutely immediate*; it is the

---

8 Malkani, op. cit., p. 14.

9 Ibid., p. 28.

10 Ibid., p. 29.

ultimate intelligent subject which can never be made our object. Malkani has nicely exemplified this notion of intelligent reality by the expression "I", and clarified this point by the fact that everybody understands what the *speaking "I"* stands for, without confusing it with any object what may be called *this*. This *speaking "I"* reveals itself for what it is and absolutely opposed to all forms of object or to *thisness*. But we very often confuse the intelligent self with forms of objectivity. That is why Malkani prefers to say "spiritual reality is a new form of reality". The knowledge of spiritual reality is self-revealing, it is not mediated by senses or thought. This kind of knowledge must be direct, immediate and indubitable. The spiritual recourse is required to attain this kind of knowledge and we can continue the spiritual course till we get to know the Absolute Truth. According to Malkani, Absolute Truth, metaphysical knowledge or *brahma-vidyā* and spiritual Intelligent Reality have been used synonymously, and also these terms explain the code of Advaita religion; Advaita religion is the religion of knowledge and not mere code of rites and rituals.

Elucidation of Advaita Doctrine

Malkani's deliberation on Advaita religion continues to link up with Advaita metaphysics. His metaphysical account is indeed a lucid elucidation of the fundamental aspect of Advaita doctrine of monism. My endeavour is to present Malkani's elucidation of principal ideas discussed in his Advaita treatise, *Metaphysics of Advaita Vedānta*. Malkani has arranged the vital issues of Advaita philosophy in the following order:

1. Advaita doctrine of monism with its general feature, indicating the criterion of distinction of real and unreal in philosophical sense,
2. Advaita concept of Ultimate Reality in the causal doctrine of Advaita metaphysics, and

3. finally, the meaning-analysis of *svarūpa lakṣaṇa* of *Brahman* as *sat–cit–ānanda*.

ADVAITA CRITERION OF REALITY

Malkani, in his treatise on Advaita metaphysics, begins with the analysis of the Advaita concept of Absolute along with a comparative account of Western Absolutism. He is primarily concerned with the formulation of the doctrine of Advaitism and especially, with the criterion for Reality, for clarification of philosophic sense of the term "Real". Accordingly, he describes how the Advaita philosophers have formulated the doctrine of Advaita monism, where all the three fundamental concepts — Truth, Reality and Knowledge — have been combined under the broad idea of the Absolute/*Brahman*. And moreover, these three ideas are not treated as different types rather all of them function in a different manner representing the one unitary metaphysical idea, *Brahman*. Naturally, this type of Absolutism has to discard the theory of manyness or pluralistic reality and restore one unitary idea as ultimately real. Hence, Advaita philosophers have started their philosophical investigation by making a philosophical distinction of real and unreal (*sat* and *a-sat*) corresponding to the Western distinction of appearance and reality, phenomena and noumena, etc. Malkani, following the Advaita criterion of truth, viz. *abādhita* (uncontradicted), marks out the fundamental distinction existing between "what is real? And what is unreal?" Needless to say that he has defined the terms "reality" and *criterion* (*abādhita*), determining the character of reality from logical standpoint. He has mentioned all the fundamental characteristics along with specific characteristics of the Reality, i.e. *Brahman*, as revealed in different verses of Upaniṣads. He has carried on the task of analysis on the basis of Upaniṣadic monistic principles of Absolute Idealism. He has not deviated from Upaniṣadic spiritualism or monism in his exposition of the review of Advaita philosophy. He has not also moulded Indian concepts after the Western model, even though he has used Western expression such as "being", "pure being" and "pure self" in his philosophical discussion; he has also construed the meaning of all these ideas related to the knowledge of *Brahman*, since *Brahman* is not unknowable. He persists to show that the knowledge of *Brahman* is accessible to *jīva* only, after the removal of ignorance. The realization of *Brahman* is possible through these two-tier process — removal of ignorance and knowing the truth. Malkani assures that the Advaita metaphysical concept of reality may not appear under the sequence of time (*trikālabādhita*), yet it never remains as unknown and unknowable idea (*aprasiddha*). Malkani has rightly observed that Advaitism is not agnosticism. He appropriately refers to *Vedānta-Sūtra*: *brahmānubhava brahmaiva bhavanti*, which signifies direct apprehension of the knowledge of *Brahman*; he has also noted down certain prescribed discipline and spiritual course to acquire the knowledge of *Brahman*.

ULTIMATE REALITY AND CAUSAL DOCTRINE

After presenting an outline of the main theme of Advaitism, he has discussed the philosophical sense of the expression "Ultimate Reality", where he characterizes *Brahman* as the *Ground*, signifying the basic fundamental principle of creation. In this context, he has given a good answer to the fundamental question: "what is Ultimate Realty?" In answering to this question, he clearly states that all the objects of the spatio-temporal world are not real, because they do not satisfy the criterion of truth, i.e. *abādhita* (uncontradicted); and because, they are changeable, variable and vulnerable, etc., and above all, they are not self-existent, all the objects come under the law of causality and under the law of relativity of things. Hence, Advaita philosophers consider the status of this type of reality as unreal; it is called phenomenal reality by Kant; and for Bradley, they are appearances; these phenomena or appearances are the limit of our knowledge. But philosophers are concerned with wider area, a search for a holistic world-view; they seek for the *ultimate cause* and cannot stop until they get at the cause which is itself uncaused, unconditional and non-relational, which somewhere must be *unrelated in itself*, so that all relations can hang on it or appear in it. Malkani concedes that the need of an unrelated and metaphysical reality is quite evident to reason as a general rule, even though reason is not a method of direct knowledge of reality; it knows reality with the aid of certain higher kind of ideas. Imminently, for the knowledge of metaphysical reality, Malkani recommends that we have to call to a super-sensible method and he refers to the revealed word (*śruti*) as the proper method for philosophical knowledge; *śruti* plays an authoritative role when all other methods of knowledge fail; *śruti* is the only way of *seeing the truth*. There are different kinds of statements in the scripture (*śruti*) which give us a knowledge of Ultimate Reality. Some statements give us indirect knowledge while others give us more direct and intimate knowledge of the basic metaphysical idea. Finally, when all our ignorance is removed, we understand the significance of great statements (*mahāvākya*s) concerning the knowledge of Ultimate Reality, the Absolute/*Brahman*. Malkani considers:

> The first stage of knowledge of metaphysical reality is to know that reality as the ultimate cause of the world or the metaphysical ground of the world.[11]

This ultimate cause can never be an effect, but an uncaused cause; it must be out of time and space.

> It is that from which all things are born, in which they stay, and into which they disappear finally (*yato-vā-imāni-bhūtāni-jayante*). *Brahman* is the cause of the birth, sustenance and end of the world.[12]

---

[11] Malkani, op. cit., pp. 35-36.

[12] Ibid., p. 36.

It has to be noted that the causality of *Brahman* is an external character or *taṭastha lakṣaṇa* of *Brahman*. According to Malkani's annotation, to say therefore, that *Brahman* is the cause of the world, is to state merely an accidental description of *Brahman*; and *Brahman* can be described as *necessary being* in a *special sense*. This expression conveys the idea of ultimate, metaphysical cause, since the world demands an ultimate metaphysical cause, that cause must transcend time, space and causality. To sum up:

> *Brahman* is the unchanging ground, while the world is a changing appearance only. The ground is the truth. It is uncreated and unborn. The world is created, and it also passes. The reality of the latter consists in name and form only, while the reality of the former is substantival. It is the same kind of relation which we find between the real and the illusory. The former is the reality of the latter. We conclude that *Brahman* is the reality of the world.[13]

The quoted lines lucidly explain the causal doctrine of Advaita indicating the causal relation between *Brahman* and the world; the world as effect has been treated as unreal because of its *vulnerable character*, even if there is substantial identity between *Brahman* as the cause and the world as effect. Malkani has also preserved the genuine idea of Advaitic monism by classifying the characteristic feature of the world as secondary, while *Brahman* as the fundamental, root cause (*causa-sui*), a sort of primodial substance from which everything comes out.

ANALYSIS OF SVARŪPA LAKṢAṆA OF BRAHMAN

In proper sequence, Malkani annotates the meaning of the component ideas of *svarūpa lakṣaṇa* of *Brahman*, otherwise known as *sat–cit–ānanda*; these three are the constituent elements constituting the defining characteristics of the concept of *Brahman*. So, in the order of descriptive analysis of the

---

13 Malkani, op. cit., p. 37.

essential attributes of *Brahman*, the concept of *sat* should get priority. Malkani has used the expressions like "Being" and "Pure Being" as substitutive ideas for the concept of *sat* and explained the meaning of this term in terms of metaphysical essence, discarding the spatio-temporal or substantial distinction (*kāla–deśa–vastu-pariccheda*). This part of *svarūpa* of *Brahman* denotes the basic idea, signifying the source of all creations; the idea of *sat*/Beings is the first category of Advaita ontology. While illustrating the salient features of this form, Malkani offers certain logical grounds for the substitutive idea of "Being" as an alternative expression of *sat*.

Sat (Being)

1. Malkani argues that "Being" is an intelligible concept and it can be known, because it signifies the common basis of all things. Moreover, the idea of Being or *sat* can never be doubted. The minute particle to the exalted form of Being, all have *sattā* or Being in the same sense. Being is the pervasive and universal locus of all things, positive entities as well as negative entities both of them are two forms of the idea of Being. It is a continuous perpetual idea, in the absence of which nothing can exist. That is why Malkani qualifies *sat* or Being as The Great.
2. Malkani has also clarified the relation between Being and worldly things in accordance with the Upaniṣadic view. It is obvious that a thing cannot be thought of without Being or *sat*; things always depend upon the locus or Being. In this sense, all things are adjectival to Being; even though, this adjectival existence is not real existence. And, because of this adjectival relation of things to the Being, all things are described as illusory, but Being sustains as the reality; Upaniṣads also admit this idea (*sarvamidam brahman*). Again, this aphorism means that *Brahman* is the only reality, and

worldly things as adjective, have no real existence; it has been better explained in another Upaniṣadic statements, viz. *neha nānāsti kiñcana*, which signifies that there is no admission of plurality in the monistic doctrine of *Brahman*. Malkani also accedes to the notion of Being as the cause of knowing the intrinsic nature of *svarūpa lakṣaṇa* of *Brahman*. According to him, in order to know *Brahman*, the idea of Being is a positive approach, since *sat* or Being is the common ground and essence of all things; we can know *Brahman* as Pure Being without any particularities and worldly differences. Malkani also concedes that the knowledge of *Brahman* as *sat* or Being is nothing mysterious.

3. Malkani also points out that the word Being does not signify any objective entity or objective situation. In this respect, it is a class by itself. For instance, when we use an empirical concept like dog, it refers to an objective entity. But when we use the concept of "cause", we know that it refers to an objective situation which can be distinguished from other objective situations not involving the concept. Similarly, the concept Being has no such reference to any particular objective situation. To confirm his argument, Malkani offers an epistemological interpretation of Being through the following illustration:

> It refers to all objects and objective situations alike, and it refers also to that unique Subject which is never an object — if we recognize any intuition which is appropriate to the latter. . . . If *A* has being, *B* has being, *C* has being, etc., then *A*, *B*, *C*, etc. are just accidents of *being*. If any of these entities is destroyed, *being* is not destroyed or affected. But without *being* as the common ground, none of these entities will ever *appear to have being*. While therefore we cannot point to something and say, "*this is being*",

> we cannot be said to have no meaning for *being*. We have the negative meaning, this, that or the other thing is *not being* or is the negation of being.[14]

The above illustration indicates that Malkani has tried to make out the philosophical significance of the concept of Being from the usage of the word "being" in different contexts of factual experiences. Further, we have to note here that the idea of Being forms the part of both real and illusory entity. The illusory entities have a *borrowed kind of Being*, not real Being.[15]

Malkani carefully notes that the attribute of *sat* (Pure Being) must not be understood to stand in any external relation to *Brahman*; *Being* does not *belong* to *Brahman* as property. Also *Being* or *sat* does not signify the manyness of the objective world, had it been so, *Being* would not constitute the essential nature of *Brahman*; there is literally a relation of identity between them; these two words *Brahman* and Being discharge two different functions with respect to one and the same thing, i.e. Reality; they are only two ways of speaking about the Reality. To quote Malkani:

> The word *Brahman* directs our attention to the ground of the world and something that is Great and Infinite, while the word *being* or *sat* directs our attention to what is eternally real and can never be cancelled in any subsequent knowledge like all things illusory. The words are different in meaning, but they coincide in significance. *Brahman* and Its *sat*-attribute stand in the relation of literal identity.[16]

Incidentally, Malkani has distinguished the Advaitic notion of Being from Hegel's notion of Being. According to Hegel, Being is the resultant concept of the process of reason. Hegel has described the notion of Being as the emptiest notion of reason. Accordingly there was a demand to develop it, in

---

14 Malkani, op. cit., p. 41.

15 Ibid., p. 42.

16 Ibid., p. 42.

order to make it adequate to the wholeness and the concreteness of Reality.

> The final form of this development was the Absolute Idea, which was the most inclusive and therefore the most stable category of Reason.[17]

While for Advaita Vedānta, as stated by Malkani, Being is to be understood not as a notion of reason but as reality itself. To the question, "what is reality in itself?" Our answer is that it is Being. Malkani has expressed the notion of Being as thing-in-itself. Being is the only thing, that is called real; to say in the words of Malkani:

> All things are made out of *being*, live in *being*, and go back to *being*. "Being" is their very stuff and substance. It is the only ultimate reality there is.[18]

Thus, Malkani ascertains that what was for Hegel the emptiest idea of reason, for Advaita Vedānta, it is the most real reality, "It is the real of all real (*satyasya satyam*)."[19]

Cit (Intelligence)

Now, we may turn over to the analysis of concept of *cit* (intelligence). As we know, pure consciousness or "pure awareness" has been used for the idea of *cit* by traditional interpreters. But Malkani translates the meaning of *cit* by an independent expression, "intelligence", because of the significant role of intelligence in the analysis of human activity, especially, human knowledge. No human activity is possible without intelligence; hence Malkani prefers the word intelligence as appropriate to explain the *svarūpa* of *Brahman* as *cit* (pure awareness). Obviously, the sense of the word intelligence used by Malkani does not carry ordinary meaning

[17] Malkani, op. cit., p. 40.

[18] Ibid.

[19] Ibid., p. 41.

of the term, which will be clear in course of our discussion. According to Malkani, the *sat*-characteristic depicts *Brahman* as unqualified Pure Being, but the idea of Pure Being cannot be understood without the idea of *cit*. Intelligence lies at the core of being; *cit* is the intrinsic character (*svarūpa Brahman*). To quote Malkani: "There can be nothing deeper or more inward in *being* than intelligence."[20] So, Malkani argues that no kind of Being have any meaning for us unless it is either associated to intelligence in knowledge; *being* and *intelligence* are inseparable, even though a distinction of intelligent being and non-intelligent being has been brought about by the Advaitins such as the distinction of *jaḍa* and *a-jaḍa*. The former signifies non-intelligent being while the latter signifies *cit* or *caitanya*. Malkani offers an argument for inseparability of Being and intelligence; he argues that since *Brahman* comprehends all Being, nothing therefore can fall outside *Brahman*, if intelligence lies beyond Being, then how can intelligence be related. Malkani, therefore, ascertains that Being is of the nature of intelligence itself; "Being that is *Brahman* is Intelligent Being".[21] In this context, Malkani refers to knowledge situation because anything to be known has to be known by intelligence, and it is an awareness of object which signifies *cit*. In knowledge, if a thing is not related to intelligence in the act of knowing, then, it is a vacuous state. Thus, a thing to be entitled to be a thing must be known, and to be known is to exist as an object of knowledge. Again, if we analyse the nature of the object of knowledge, it will be found that every object is qualified by these two essential characteristics, viz. its Being (*sattā*) and awareness of it, i.e. *cit*, and *Brahman* comprehends both the idea of *sat* and *cit*. Hence, Malkani describes *Brahman* as an Intelligent Being.

---

[20] Malkani, op. cit., p. 43.

[21] Ibid., p. 44.

Malkani, while explaining the notion of *cit* as intelligence, raises a pertinent question, "what sort of intelligence is this"? Providing an answer to this question, Malkani categorically says that *cit* as *svarūpa* of *Brahman* does not signify finite human intelligence. As we know human mental functions operated through intelligence are called *vr̥tti* in Advaita terminology. On the other hand, "intelligence" when used as a substitutive idea for *cit*, it bears a different meaning. Here *cit* signifies Pure Awareness. As we have seen that the expression Pure Being has been used for *sat*, similarly the expression "pure formless awareness" or "pure intelligence" has been used by Malkani for the expression of *cit*. Malkani, further, elaborates this point by the function of intelligence in cognitive activity; *cit* reveals upon individual knower; that is why Malkani calls it "borrowed intelligence" reflected in finite human beings. Malkani has rightly observed that "pure intelligence" or "pure awareness" is the basic idea in knowledge, which is also known as *sākṣī caitanya*; but it cannot operate by itself since it is an abstract idea; *sākṣī* functions in and through the medium of individual knower (*pramātā*).

Now, Malkani finds a difficulty in correlating the idea of *cit* or pure intelligence with that of finite intelligent act. The expression pure intelligence cannot be explained without the concept of individual knower, since human mind is a series of intelligent activity and also an intelligent cognitive agent. So it appears that the expression "pure intelligence" does not have any application in reality without the medium of finite intelligence; it is "an idea only". At the same time, the pure intelligence as a general idea conducts all sorts of intelligent act of finite minds. Hence, Malkani makes a cryptic remark:

> Thus pure intelligence is a myth, while the intelligent act is a reality.[22]

---

[22] Malkani, op. cit., pp. 45-46.

However, Malkani does not leave this issue as mere myth. He tries to dissolve this problem through the analysis of empirical knowledge. When a sensible object is known, the knower of it cannot be known; the act of knowledge qualifies the knower, in this way, knower is known. The knower *as such* is never known. But to know the knower, we require another qualified knower. Again, this knower is not simultaneous with the one, it is supposed to know; further, the later, in time, cannot know the earlier. So, Malkani resolves this distinction between knower and the known as absolute. The knower can never be the known. Malkani apprehends the knower as an actless awareness or pure intelligence; that is the true subject, and it is never an object; it is *cit* (pure awareness), also called *śuddha-caitanya* in Advaita terminology.

The idea of pure awareness is the fundamental principle of knowledge conducting the activity of individual knower. In other words, pure intelligence reveals upon the individual subject, because pure *cit* in knowledge situation cannot know an object as object. In any cognitive act of human mind, there is a higher level of awareness which is pure intelligence; this pure intelligence functions through the active knower (*pramātā*) in different cognitive acts. And we can directly know a cognitive act of mind through *pramātā* (individual knower). Here, Malkani points out that even though pure intelligence is not directly involved in any cognitive activity, it stands between the individual knower and the object of knowledge in a relation of false identity (*adhyāsic tādātmya*), which is not a real relation. And in this process, Pure intelligence knows the world as the ultimate knower. This ultimate knower (*cit*) does not require any intermediate mental act (*vṛtti*); it reveals the subject and subject–object correlationship; it stands only in relation of false identity. Malkani has summarized the idea of pure *cit* as the ultimate knower or the basic principles of all knowledge in the following lines:

> To sum up, when I know *x*, *x* is the object and I am the knower. When I know this knower (*pramātā*), the knower is the object while that which knows it is pure awareness. This pure awareness or pure intelligence is the ultimate term in all knowledge. It is *before* all cognition that arises, as well as *after* it. It itself does not arise. It reveals not only the arisen act, but also its prior non-existence and its posterior non-existence. It knows without being known in its turn.[23]

This is how, Malkani comprehends the distinction of individual subject and pure awareness (*śuddha-caitanya*) as "functional only, not substantial". Malkani interprets pure intelligence as "True Subject", which cannot be related to object as it is formless awareness. Since pure awareness *as such* cannot operate in factual cases of knowledge, it operates through the individual subject in different contexts of knowledge; pure intelligence is the ground of knowledge. Malkani considers individual subject as superficial; while pure intelligence is the real subject.

> The latter is of nature of pure intelligence. It is the ground of all appearances, both objective and subjective. It is the ultimate metaphysical reality.[24]

Now, Malkani has reversed to the question of understanding the meaning of pure intelligence as the self (*ātman*). Since there is a difficulty in expressing this metaphysical idea of *cit*, Malkani intends to take a resort to metaphorical or suggestive language, which points out the way of understanding this concept. Malkani, therefore, attempts to explain the meaning of pure intelligence by analysing the negative aspect of pure intelligence in different ways, such as, pure intelligence is not an entity, which we can directly know; or we may say that pure intelligence is the negation of every thing that is unintelligent (*jaḍa*). Thus, Malkani concedes that pure intelligence can be best understood by negative way:

---

23 Malkani, op. cit., p. 47.

24 Ibid., p. 49.

> Here negation is possible and can be carried to its farthest limit. This limit is reached when *everything objective* and *everything that can confront us* is negated and what is left is the formless awareness that sustains all forms. Some knowledge of the intelligent reality is thus possible through a thorough-going negation.[25]

Malkani, after elaborate analysis of the meaning of pure *cit*, concludes that *cit* like *sattā* constitutes the intrinsic characteristics of *Brahman*; and they are not external to *Brahman*. Malkani has rightly observed that Being and Intelligence (*sat* and *cit*) have been tied up by the relation of identity. It is one and the same thing called by different names. The names have different functions to perform. They direct our attention in different ways, and thus enable us to reject certain characters from the nature of reality. Malkani precisely puts his view:

> "*Brahman*" rejects what is finite, "Being" rejects what is illusory, and "Intelligence" rejects what is un-intelligent or *jaḍa*. In this way they dispel different kinds of doubt and different forms of misconception about the nature of ultimate reality. In the end, they meet in the same reality, and are indistinguishable from one another. "*Brahman* is described as *nirvikāra — citi-rev-akevala* (i.e., pure formless intelligence)".[26]

Ānanda (Bliss)

Keeping in conformity with Upaniṣadic deliberation, Malkani has described the nature of *sat–cit–ānanda Brahman* as intelligent being and spiritual in character. Inevitably, the concept of *ānanda*, the category of value, comes up for elucidation; *ānanda* contributes as a significant part of the structure of the Absolute in Advaita Vedānta. This concept reveals the complete sense

---

[25] Malkani, op. cit., p. 50.

[26] Ibid., p. 51.

of *Brahman* as the highest metaphysical idea, comprising the idea of *Brahman* as the Supreme Being (*sat*), *Brahman* as the Supreme Knowledge (*cit*) and *Brahman* as the abode of Supreme Value (*ānanda*); Malkani has presented the annotation of *sat* and *cit* indicating the interrelation between them. So, in the chronological order, Malkani annotates the meaning of this value concept of *ānanda*. He has displayed the natural transition from being to intelligence (*sat* to *cit*), representing ontological and epistemological aspect of Advaita metaphysics and illustrated how "Being is intelligent in itself". Now, he raises a pertinent question: "is there any transition from Being to value?", because the nature of Being as a neutral idea does not imply value. At the same time, the category of value cannot be separated from intelligent being; intelligent being cannot but be pleasurable or painful being. To make this point clear, Malkani has discussed the distinctive features of finite joy and infinite joy. According to him, the true sense of the state of joy of Being is "intrinsically valuable state" and this joy is not the means to some end. "It is the only thing that is unconditionally valuable".[27] But finite intelligent being always in a state, either pleasurable or painful, happy or unhappy, there may be apparently a neutral state. Pleasure, pain, happy, unhappy, etc. are different states of finite being with a motivation. But *ānanda* signifies the state of enjoying eternal bliss/infinite joy, otherwise known as the state of *turīya* or *mokṣa*, the highest ideal in Advaita philosophy.

Further, Malkani has clarified the significance of this value concept, *ānanda* from moral standpoint. In this context, Malkani discusses some moral values to bring out the distinguishing feature of *ānanda* as eternal bliss. He has also marked out the difference between human values and Advaita value concept, on the basis of the analysis of moral action. In this assessment,

---

27 Malkani, op. cit., p. 52.

Malkani has emphasized that the aesthetic satisfaction gives us pleasure, but it sustains as a mere feeling; on the other hand, in moral acts, feeling or emotion does not play a significant role, because we have to dispassionately judge an act to be right or wrong, in judging morality of action. Emotion comes in the later phase of action when we approve or disapprove any moral act. Thus, the approval or disapproval is the consequent upon moral judgement; it cannot convert the act into moral or immoral, and moral judgement or moral value is a matter of evaluation. Again, evaluation is related to our fundamental needs like, desire, aspiration, etc. So, evaluation in most cases is dominated by subjective factors, even though moral act is performed purely from the sense of duty. This kind of duty is not a cognitive matter, according to Malkani, it is a "matter of will". Contrarily, the joy which is implied in the concept of *ānanda,* is pure spiritual enlightenment opposed to the finite joy of self-fulfilment. This infinite joy has been described in Upaniṣad as "That which is Great is full of joy; the small is painful (*yo-wai-bhūmā-tat-sukham, nālpe sukhamasti*)".[28]

In this connection, Malkani has pointed out the limitations of the finite. Correspondingly, he has also given the details of the recommendation of the Advaitins to get rid of the limitations of finitude, such as the limitation of birth, death, diseases and all sorts of human bondage, so that he can enjoy the Highest joy (*ānanda*). Accordingly, Malkani has noted down the spiritual courses through which an individual can attain this Highest state and enjoy infinite joy only when he is free from the chain of birth and death (*asaṁsārī*), and eternally free from every kind of bondage (*nitya mukta*). This state is known as *amr̥tam* signifying immortality. In this way, Malkani tries to show the application of the concept of *ānanda* in the

[28] Malkani, op. cit., p. 54.

life of an individual (*jīva*). He ensures that *jīva* can attain the state of immortality (*amṛtam*).

Malkani also marks out a difference between the objective value and the spiritual value. When an object of desire fulfils the desire of a person, he gets satisfaction or joy; his objective desire being fulfilled is called the objective value, which is not the ultimate goal or spiritual value in the life of an individual. According to Advaita moral code, Real joy is a spiritual attainment leading to a painless state and free from all sorts of objective limits. The Real joy (*ānanda*) specifically "is characterized by equanimity, poise and peace. It is a state of desirelessness. There is no enjoyer in it, and nothing enjoyed. It is the joy that more nearly approximates to the joy of non-duality."[29] Further, Malkani explains the qualitative difference between the finite joy and the infinite joy or eternal bliss (*ānanda*). He specifically mentions:

> The joy of *Brahman* is qualitatively different from all other joys. It has no negative side. It is purely positive. There is no desire and no fulfilment of desire. It is the joy of *being*. Being itself is bliss. There are joys which are the products of inner pressures and outer fortune. The bliss of *Brahman* is different from them all. It is the *own nature* of *Brahman*. To know *Brahman* is therefore to know It as blissful. If we presumably know *Brahman*, but do not feel the bliss of *Brahman*, it is not genuine knowledge of *Brahman* at all. Knowledge and bliss are here inseparable.[30]

The above remarks of Malkani clearly show that the infinite joy, *ānanda* (bliss) is the characteristic feature of *brahma-jñāna*; *ānanda* is not merely an aesthetic value. On the other hand, *ānanda* is the spiritual joy derived from the knowledge of non-duality, *Brahman*; the joy created by *ānanda* is called the positive

---

[29] Malkani, op. cit., p. 55.

[30] Ibid.

joy. Malkani describes the nature of *positive joy* in the following manner:

> The only positive joy is the wantless and desireless joy that is in the very nature of *being*. To be *is* to be joyful. *It is this joy that is being, that expresses itself positively in all other joys that are desire-based*. . . . When the pain or the desire is removed, the fundamental and ever-present joy of being manifests itself. It is never really lost. It only appears to be lost and regained.[31]

Malkani completes his review of the concept of *ānanda* by making a sharp contrast of objective value with subjective value. Since, the objective value cannot yield higher type of spiritual element, it has been sub-graded. The real joy or spiritual enlightenment lies not in the object but in the *self*. We wrongly locate joy in the object. Malkani, therefore, suggests that we should not give importance to the objective value, rather we should try to experience unity with the self (*ātman)*; the highest joy is the joy of non-duality of *jīva* and *Brahman*. Malkani also anticipates that the joy of non-duality cannot be conceived when we are engrossed with mundane pleasure. He believes:

> The infinite joy lies deep down in our own being. We can know this joy only when we know our being to be the being of *Brahman*. This is the knowledge of unity of the individual (*jīva*) and the Absolute.[32]

When *jīva* acquires this knowledge of non-duality, it realizes that "the joy of *Brahman* is infinite, pure, positive and without end".[33] In this state of *ānanda*, *jīva*/individual recognizes its identity with *Brahman*. Finite being, when feels this feeling of unity with *Brahman*, it reaches the Highest end and becomes

---

31 Malkani, op. cit., p. 57.

32 Ibid., p. 58.

33 Ibid.

free (*mukta*) and this is the state of infinite joy (*ānanda*). So, the concept of *ānanda* is not only a part of the ontological structure of *Brahman*, but it also indicates the way for the realization of the Highest goal of human life. Evidently, *ānanda* plays a very significant role in organizing human activities and moulding human life suitable for attaining the highest goal of life. To say precisely, *ānanda* functions in the Advaita doctrine as a guiding principle of human life, as a code of moral conduct and, finally, prepares the finite being for the attainment of *mokṣa* (liberation).

In sequel to this work, Malkani turns to a new dimension of the attributes of *Brahman*. He has sorted out positive attributes signifying *being*, *intelligence* and *bliss* (*sat–cit–ānanda*), and the negative attributes, signifying the accompanying characteristics of *Brahman*, such as infinitude (*anantam*). The latter one has been regarded as negative because it can be understood negatively. "Infinity" comes up in the trail of sequence of positive attributes, as a follow-up idea of the concept of *being*; there is an inseparable metaphysical link between *being* and infinite, even though infinity has been considered as a negative attribute, because it is known as opposite to finite. Moreover, Infinity connotes specific qualities such as non-spatial and non-temporal. Eventually, Malkani reduces both the attributes under one form, since any attribute can only be interpreted in objective language referring to the object of experience, and objective language cannot convey the literal meaning of the word *Brahman*. So, he recommends for an intellectual intuition of *Brahman* and prefers the use of a symbolic expression for this purpose. However, he has compromised on the difference of positive and negative attributes in the following comprehensive remark:

> All the attributes of *Brahman*, both positive and negative, point to one and the same thing, that is without any differences in it. It is spoken differently and described

differently. The function of this description is not to introduce differences, where none obtain, but to point to the unique and indivisible character of the reality that is *Brahman*. The thing is one. We call it, for the convenience of our understanding, by different names.[34]

Identity of Jīva and Brahman

Following the order of natural sequence in metaphysical discourse, Malkani enunciates the non-duality of *Brahman* and simultaneously enumerates the identity of *jīva* with *Brahman*. He has pronounced this relation of identity in definite terms and illustrated through the factual illustration of knowledge such as "I know you" and "I know *X*". The epistemological analysis of these statements shows the function of two basic ideas: subject, as a knower and the object. Malkani explains the function of the basic ideas in knowledge indicating distinct character of subject, "I", as a speaker and "you" as the person spoken to; the knowledge of "I" is direct, immediate and known directly as the first person, whereas all other persons like "you" and "he" are some kind of object interpreted by the "I" which are considered to be copies or imitations of "I", known on the basis of analogy. So, these two different types of idea have to be unified under one "whole" to fulfil the requirement of the Ultimate Reality. Malkani finds the problem of unity, to be brought about between the subject and the object joining together under a frame of one whole. So, he apprehends that there must be a comprehensive and all-inclusive absolute experience comprising all the ideas of subject and object, where all differences are dissolved under one unitary idea. Malkani found that Advaitins formulated the theory of identity of *jīva* and *Brahman* in the same language. According to Advaitins, *Brahman/ātman* is the basis of all descriptions about the individual subject "I"; every instance

[34] Malkani, op. cit., p. 62.

of "I" presupposes this concept of *ātman* (self), the ultimate subject known as Absolute Spirit. It is evident that the idea of *jīva* is contained in the universal idea of ultimate subject or Self. Thus *jīva* is construed to be indistinguishable from the Self or *Ātman* and *jīva* has to recognize the feeling of non-duality.

From the epistemological analysis, Malkani expounded the metaphysical theory of the relation between *jīva* (the individual self) and the concept of *ātman*. Malkani gives the details about how *jīva* acquires the knowledge of the essential attribute (*svarūpa lakṣaṇa*) of *Brahman* and how this knowledge brings about literal identity of *jīva* with *Brahman*; how *jīva* as a spiritual entity directly knows its identity (*tat-tvam-asi*). In this stage, *jīva* reaches the apex of supreme value and realizes its identity with *Brahman* (*aham brahmāsmi*). This highest knowledge of unity with *Brahman* occurs only after the removal of *jīva*'s ignorance; *jīva* has to accrue this knowledge of unity as an eternal relation; *jiva* is not a separate entity, only an existing entity seeming different from *Brahman*. Malkani cites an instance of similar type of wrong identification, viz. "This is that Devadutta, I have seen in Banaras". This instance shows how the same person seen in two occasions may be confused as two different persons. But we should not count two Devaduttas, seen in two different places. In point of truth, there is one person with the same identity. Similarly, *Brahman* appearing different from *jīva*, and this feeling of difference has been created by *jīva*'s ignorance. When ignorance is removed, *jīva* feels its oneness with *Brahman*/*ātman*; *jīva* comprehends this eternal identity and achieves the supreme goal of life (*mokṣa*).

Here Malkani very carefully notes that *jīva*'s knowledge of unity with *Brahman* is not judgemental, it is not even a new acquisition in knowledge; it is only a recognition of identity which was left to be recovered; *jīva* has to practise some spiritual discipline to qualify himself for this spiritual attainment. Now Malkani mentions certain spiritual course prescribed by the Advaitins. *Jīva* must observe those spiritual disciplines for the realization of truth (*brahma-jñāna*). In accordance with the spiritual course, *jīva* must learn discernment and follow spiritual life as prescribed in the code of Dharmaśāstra (concerning action prescribed by scripture) and Mokṣaśāstra (the part concerning knowledge of Truth, which Malkani calls the metaphysical knowledge). After the successful completion of spiritual practices, *jīva* is considered to be competent for the recognition and realization of its identity with *Brahman*, the concealed identity appears as revealed. Malkani nicely remarks on *jīva's* revealed identity:

> When we do so, two substances do not become one. There is only one real substance which has appeared to us under two different names and two different forms. *Jīva* and *Brahman* have literal identity.[35]

To explain this state of *jīva*, Malkani adds:

> Only our ignorance of this identity is removed. That alone introduces a sort of novelty and a sense of achievement in our knowledge. In point of fact, we only know what we already knew in a way in our own being.[36]

To say otherwise, *jīva* becomes aware that it was unaware of its identity with *Brahman*.

To end up, I wish to highlight some significant features of Malkani's excellence in the orientation of Advaitism as a synthesis of philosophy and religion. No doubt, Malkani is one of the chief exponents of classical interpretation of Advaitavāda in contemporary vocabulary and he has presented his thesis in an intelligible manner. The foregoing analysis reveals that Malkani stands out conspicuous and distinct in respect of his interpretation of Advaita Vedānta.

---

35 Malkani, op. cit., p. 74.

36 Ibid., p. 73.

The uniqueness of his analysis consists in showing how philosophy and religion share a common protasis not only in respect of method of knowledge, but also in the knowledge of truth. Advaita philosophy and theology adopt the a-rational method of intuition for comprehension of Ultimate Truth, which is supra-rational. Malkani defines Advaita religion as the religion of knowledge. Accordingly, he has explained how Advaitavāda postulates the ground for higher knowledge and consequently, how religious pursuit culminates in the highest form of knowledge or Absolute Truth. Subsequently, he attempts to show that Advaita philosophy and Advaita religion have been integrated in the wide spectrum of monistic doctrine of Advaita Vedānta.

The non-dualistic strain in Malkani's interpretation can hardly be overemphasized though it came to be questioned by K.S. Murty. *Brahman* is posited as the ultimate "world-ground" (*causa-sui*). Though *Brahman* is indeterminable in terms of categories, it remains intelligible only in terms of *sat*, *cit* and *ānanda*, which have been construed as Being, Intelligence, Bliss, a spiritual value, respectively; the novelty of his annotation of the constitutive ideas is worth-noting. Also, Malkani elucidates the notion of individual self in his inimical style. Though individual self, *jīva* partakes of the nature of *Brahman*, on account of ignorance, it remains under the illusion of being an isolated existential entity. Truth is attained, only when the veil of ignorance is removed by self-effort through such spiritual discipline as *vairāgya*, *śravaṇa*, *manana* and *nididhyāsana*, and all duties prescribed by the scripture have got to be performed disinterestedly in order to earn the qualification and the desire for the knowledge of *Brahman* (*mumukṣa*). But such knowledge of truth does not mean acquisition of new knowledge, but the recognition of pristine truth of which one was unaware due to self-courted ignorance.

3

Critique of Advaitism — K.S. Murty

K.S. MURTY is one of the few luminaries who shine by their own light. He stands out conspicuous for offering a unique interpretation of the Advaita text. *Revelation and Reason in Advaita Vedānta* is indisputably his *magnum opus* which reveals Murty as a critique of Advaitism. In view of the wide spectrum addressed by Murty, I would confine myself to the nature and criterion of reality, i.e. *Brahman* and the method of attaining *Brahman*-knowledge. My analysis shall tend to show that Murty's criticism of non-dualism is not tenable. Murty has underlined the definition of *Brahman* as *satyam, jñānam* and *anantam* (truth, knowledge, infinity), and has sought to show that they are logically integral and central to the understanding of *Brahman*. While dilating upon the methodology or means of *Brahman*-realization, he construes *anubhava* and revelation as the fundamental and reason as auxiliary. He contends that the very concept of revelation is contrary to the spirit of non-dualism or absolute monism because it entails the distinction between the revealer and the recipient of revelation. I shall be making a humble attempt to give an exposition of Murty's analysis of the notion of Advaita followed by my critique of his viewpoint.

Definition of Brahman: Annotation

Murty has presented an illuminating analysis of the concept of *Brahman*, the Absolute in Advaita Vedānta, in his book *Revelation and Reason in Advaita Vedānta*. In this chapter I intend to dwell upon Murty's annotation of the Upaniṣadic definition of *Brahman*, viz. *satyam, jñānam* and *anantam*. In course of discussion it will be clear that Murty's primary concern is to present a logical definition of *Brahman*; he has explained the meaning of these attributive words attributed to *Brahman* both from etymological standpoint and logical standpoint. Virtually Murty, in expounding the meaning of the Advaita concept, has presented an elaborate critique of Advaitism. He has stressed much upon the efficacy of language to be used for defining the concept of *Brahman*. In this regard, he has settled the issue referring to Śaṅkara's viewpoint.

Murty begins his analysis of the concept with the significance of the word *Brahman* in the chapter "Language and Brahman". It has to be noted here that he has made a good effort to clarify the meaning of the concept of *Brahman* by etymological analysis used in contemporary philosophical method. The novelty of his philosophical approach is to bring about a compromise between logical and etymological rules, keeping the metaphysical character of the concept of Absolute/*Brahman* uninjured. He has not reduced the fundamental characteristics of Advaita monism to mere linguistic form. Rather Murty's philosophical analysis brings about a reconciliation between syntactical and semantical aspects of the word *Brahman*.

Now let us explore the significance of the word *Brahman* following the contemporary logico-linguistic method adopted by Murty. Against the linguistic background, he has narrated different types of language; he has talked of empirical language, scientific language and their relevance to commonsense objective language. In this connection, Murty has raised an interesting sceptical question in respect of empirical relevance of "*Brahman*-language".

> How are we to understand the word *Brahman* occurring in the Upaniṣads? And why would a man *desire* at all to know

Brahman, which he has not come across in experience?[1]

In answering to these questions, Murty has referred to Upaniṣadic text and asserts that *Brahman* can be known by the study of the Veda, i.e. in Vedic terms. So, one who has studied Veda, will understand the essential nature of *Brahman*, because empirical language is incompetent to describe *Brahman*. But Murty points out that there are certain words, citing the example of heaven, which is not an empirical word but we understand the meaning of this word in the context of common usage. In the same way, the meaning of the word *Brahman* becomes clearer when we observe the syntactical connection of this word with other familiar words in Vedic sentences, because, meaning of a word becomes clear with reference to its contextual usages. Murty analyses the meaning from the root of the word *Brahman* and displays how it is derived from the idea of greatness, and how the structure of the word has been composed by combining *Brah* and *man*, the former signifying "the great". The meaning of the expression "the great" has been elaborated in these lines:

> Etymologically, *Brahman* is derived from a root which signifies "greatness" and unsurpassed greatness, because no other words or topic limit that sense. So we further know that *Brahman* is free from the limitations of space, time and things.[2]

And moreover, Murty extends the meaning-analysis of "greatness" by the application of the word, common case, such as, when it is predicated of persons, who excel others in genius or power, and are free from the shortcomings of others. By this simile, Murty confirms that *Brahman* being the greatest thing of all, cannot have any defects such as "limited

---

1 K.S. Murty, *Revelation and Reason in Advaita Vedānta*, Delhi: Motilal Banarsidass, 1974, p. 53.

2 Ibid., p. 54.

substantiality" and "inertness" and therefore the attributive word "great" signifies the highest end. Murty acknowledges that when a conception so arrived at, through etymology, indicates that only the existence of such thing is possible (*sambhāvanā mātra-buddhi*). And once we know that the existence of such a thing is possible, then we can begin an investigation about it. Because any discussion (*vicāra*) is possible about a conceivable thing (*pratipanna vastu*), but not about something inconceivable such as a barren woman's son. This word involves self-contradiction whereas the conception of *Brahman* involves no such contradiction; *Brahman* can be known, *Brahman* is knowable (*prasiddha*) and it is not unknowable or an obscure thing, for the Upaniṣad says that "*Brahman* is this self (*ayam ātma Brahman*)"[3] and in the form "I am", the self is evident to the whole world (*sarvaloka pratyakṣa*), *Brahman* is not entirely unknown (*atyanta aprasiddhi abhavat*). Murty, therefore, concedes:

> The Advaitins say that he, who studies the Veda and knows the meanings of the words from etymology and grammar, gets an idea of eternal *Brahman* from texts, such as "the Real" alone was in the beginning; "that thou art", etc.[4]

Murty's assertion clearly shows that all scriptural statements have been formulated on the basis of etymology and grammar, and Veda is the source of the knowledge of *Brahman*.

It is worth to note that Murty as a critique of Advaita points out the possibility of the logical oddness of the meaning of the word *Brahman* by referring to the paradox of *Brahman*-sentences in Vedānta. In this regard, Murty raised a controversial point:

> How can the Vedānta sentences have their object *Brahman*, which is said to be the eternal subject?

---

[3] Murty, op. cit., p. 55.

[4] Ibid.

Murty resolves this problem referring to Śaṅkara's view on this point:

> The reply of Śaṅkara is that the Upaniṣads do not indicate *Brahman* as the "this" — an object — to be known by us. . . . The Upaniṣads inform us that *Brahman* is not an object (*aviṣaya*), since it is the inner self (*pratyagātmā*).[5]

So Murty makes it clear that Upaniṣadic sentences teach that *Brahman* does not signify a particular object as "this" or "that" and negate all adjuncts to *Brahman*; the word *Brahman* is equivalent to "the great" and *ātman* (equivalent to "the self"); these two etymologically indicate the idea of *Brahman*, because, "it is self-luminous and all-pervasive".[6]

Murty also refers to Śaṅkara's *Gītā Bhāṣya* where Śaṅkara discusses the relationship between language and *Brahman* and comments that *Brahman* is incapable of being related to words:

> *Brahman* cannot be described by the word *is* nor by the words *is not*, for it is super-sensual, it is not the object of knowledge in the form "is" or "is not" (*ubhaya buddhi anugata pratyaya aviṣayatvāt*).[7]

Brahman is neither "being" nor "non-being", because *Brahman* is incapable of being related to words, because all words are related to certain reference; and it is possible to relate words to their referent either through space, action, quality or connection.

Since *Brahman* has no quality and is actionless, it cannot be qualified or spoken of as doing something. It is also unconnected with anything, because It is the sole reality without a second; since It is never the object, but is always the self, It is but proper that no words can signify It and the Upaniṣads also confirm this (*Taittirīya Up.* II.4-9).[8] Hence Murty

5 Murty, op. cit., p. 56.

6 Ibid., p. 57.

7 Ibid., p. 58.

8 Ibid., p. 59.

finds difficulty in the linguistic expression of the word *Brahman* and holds that verbal analysis is inadequate to explain the meaning of *Brahman*, yet finite beings has to use language to express the idea of *Brahman*, and also by attributing *Brahman* by language, such as

> *Brahman* has hands, legs, eyes, heads, faces, and ears on all sides; encompassing all, it stands.[9]

According to Śaṅkara, these false attributions enable us to comprehend *Brahman*'s existence and Murty refers to Śaṅkara's view to resolve the problem of description of *Brahman* in language and holds:

> Once *Brahman* is posited as the supreme self, the problem of its description arises, and then from the Upaniṣads and our own reasoning we learn that all human concepts, derived from man's experience of objective things in space and time, are inadequate to describe *Brahman*. But as long as one inquires about *Brahman*, words have to be used about it; but in order that the limitations of human concepts may be brought out, and the nature of *Brahman* revealed somehow through this odd and logically inappropriate language, an *adhyāropa*, i.e. a false attribution, *is* first made of *Brahman*, and then an *apavāda* or negation of this is made. For instance, if *Brahman* is first described as it is "many footed and many handed", immediately this is rejected, and if it is described as "it moves" in the very next sentence this is denied.[10]

Thus, Murty finds the clue in the methods of *adhyāropa* and *apavāda* to grasp the truth by being led through a false path. Accordingly,

> the conclusion is that words used for describing *Brahman* are not to be understood univocally, according to the usual material mode of talking, for they at best attempt to describe

---

9 Murty, op. cit., p. 59.

10 Ibid.

> a mystery which exceeds them and we use them because "one cannot keep silent".[11]

All these lines, clearly show that Murty is primarily concerned with logical analysis of the metaphysical concept to make it intelligible. In the above-quoted passage, it is also implied that since *Brahman* is super-sensual, it cannot be described by objective language; language is inadequate and all the description of *Brahman* has been attributed to him through *adhyāropa* (false attribution) and by *apavāda* (which means negation). However these false attributions or adjuncts attributed to *Brahman* help us to comprehend the "*Brahman*-existence". Murty, therefore, accepts that *Brahman* can only be apprehended by means of scripture.

Now, we shall enter into the discussion from etymological analysis to ontological analysis on the basis of Upaniṣadic definition of *Brahman* — *satyam, jñānam* and *anantam*. "The definition per essentiam" of *Brahman* is "reality, knowledge and infinity".[12] According to Murty's annotation of this definition of *Brahman*, the terms "reality", "knowledge", etc. are used as adjectives of *Brahman*, because according to Śaṅkara, these adjectives are primarily meant for definition (*lakṣaṇa*). Murty has marked out that adjectives differentiate a thing from other thing of its class only, whereas *lakṣaṇa*s differentiate it from all things. These *lakṣaṇa*s do not connote contingent or accidental characteristics of *Brahman* (*taṭastha lakṣaṇa*), but constitute the essential characteristics (*svarūpa lakṣaṇa*) of *Brahman*; these essential characteristics of *Brahman* are not mutually related. So each of them is related to the word *Brahman* independently of the others, i.e. "reality is *Brahman*", "knowledge is *Brahman*" and "infinity is *Brahman*".[13]

---

11 Murty, op. cit., p. 60.

12 Ibid., p. 4.

13 Ibid., p. 61.

> The words "reality", "knowledge" and "infinity" have, no doubt, different meanings; but they refer to one indivisible thing, because their purport is unity. Each of them respectively negates unreality, materiality and multiplicity. The negation of multiplicity does not raise any problem, because multiplicity, which is not describable either as real or unreal, cannot affect the absolute reality of non-duality.[14]

Murty has also referred to the remark of the Advaitin, Vidyāraṇya regarding this definition. According to Vidyāraṇya's interpretation; "Reality, knowledge and infinity are *Brahman*"; the words "reality", etc. have their own different general meanings, but as used here all of them have one impartite sense.[15] Murty has illustrated these ideas, viz. *satyam, jñānam, anantam,* in the chronological order for better understanding of this conceptual trio, in respect of Advaita ontology. I shall try to present the meaning of the words *satyam, jñānam* and *anantam* following the annotation given by Murty.

Satyam (Reality)

Murty refers to the statement: "Reality is *Brahman*", for the elucidation of the concept of *sat/satyam,* because the word *sat* has been used in various senses such as "reality", "being", "existence" and "truth", all of them designate the idea of *sat/ satyam*. Murty brings out the ontological implication in this concept and ascertains that though the monistic thinkers maintain that the fundamental principle underlying all diversities is one and the same, they have divergent views on the conception of reality/*sat*. These divergent views are expressed in various forms, in different contexts. Therefore, in the analysis of the word "reality", following Śaṅkara's interpretation of it, Murty substantiates:

---

14 Murty, op. cit., p. 65.

15 Ibid., p. 66.

> According to Śaṅkara, "reality" is that which does not deviate from its ascertained nature, while unreality is change (*vikāra*). As the Upaniṣads have explained, "Being" without change is reality.[16]

Besides, Murty illustrates the meaning of the word "reality" in the context of normal usages such as when a thing is known to have a certain definite form and that form never fails to accompany the thing is known as real, when on the other hand, a thing first found to have one form and then asserted to have another form, the philosophers consider it to be unreal, as it is changeable by nature. So, in the vulnerable phase of empirical knowledge, concepts are not absolutely true. Hence, philosophers consider them to be phenomenal and not real in absolute sense. Murty continues to elaborate the significance of the word "reality" from metaphysical usages in Advaita. He finds that the term "reality" in Advaita literature appears in various forms such as *nitya, nirākāra* and *satya/sat*. Accordingly, Murty clarifies the meaning of these concepts from Advaitic standpoint. The Advaitins describe the conception of eternity as *nitya* in two forms, viz. *kūṭastha nitya* and *pariṇāmī nitya*. The word *kūṭastha nitya* as interpreted by Murty means the austerity in determining the nature of truth or reality. The idea of *kūṭastha,* specifically characterized by Murty, is an incorrigible idea. The other form of *nitya,* viz. *pariṇāmī nitya,* also conforms to the criterion of incorrigibility, but with a relaxation, i.e. "transformation", as happens in case of *prakṛti pariṇāmavāda*. The idea of *pariṇāmī nitya* entertains the idea of transformation, though eternal basically.

Murty has introduced another idea, viz. *pravāharūpa nityatā* as a substitute for *pariṇāmī nitya* and has arranged these concepts in the following order:

---

16 Murty, op. cit., p. 61.

> A thing is *kūṭastha nitya* if it is unchanged for ever, while a thing has *pravāharūpa nityatā* if though incessantly changing it does not alter its pattern (*niyati*). Roughly speaking, a rock, for example, has the former kind of reality, and a river the latter kind. The nature of a river is to flow incessantly, and so long as it does not swerve from this nature of its, it may be said to be "mutably real"; though not "enduringly real" as a rock.[17]

Thus, Murty accords to the "enduring" aspect as the fundamental characteristics of the notion of reality including the idea of essence or the source, out of which various sprouts come out, known as name and form (*nāma-rūpa*). But the fundamental basis, out of which name and form originate, is formless and nameless, that is called *nirākāra*. This word *nirākāra* plays a most significant part in the Advaita conception of *Brahman* (*yat nirākāra tat sat*). Murty has very appropriately placed the notion of *nirākāra* distinguishing it from *sākāra*. He rightly observes that the basic concept cannot be *sākāra*, because *sākāra* can be understood in terms of space and time; it has to be manifested only through the contingent facts and contingency disqualifies the notion of eternity. Therefore, reality has been described as *nirākāra* to fulfil the logical requirement of metaphysical characteristics.

Moreover, according to Advaita criterion of truth, these terms, *sat, nitya,* etc. comply with the meaning of eternity as the essential features of reality and it is identical with the notion of truth, because reality cannot be untrue. While describing the nature of reality, the first question arises "How do we distinguish and determine the nature of the real and the unreal". It is an important philosophical question. So a criterion is needed to determine the nature of *nitya* and *anitya* (real and unreal) and to discriminate the nature of reality (*sat*) from the nature of unreality. The Advaitins follow the principle

---

17 Murty, op. cit., p. 40.

of *abādhita* (uncontradicted) as the criterion of truth and reality and they have accepted only the Vedic knowledge as uncontradicted. Murty also accedes to the Advaita view and expresses in clear terms:

> The Veda is a reliable authority, because it teaches us about things which are highly useful (*phalavat*) and are not known otherwise (*anādhigata*); and this knowledge is uncontradicted (*abādhita*).[18]

It may be added here that Murty has mentioned some other concepts like *viśuddha sattā* and *pāramārthika sattā* in typical Advaitic sense. Here, Murty has used *sattā* and *sat* interchangeably. *Pāramārthika sattā* is not subject to changing conditions, and which is equivalent to the philosophical sense of truth. This truth is one, eternal (*nitya*), pure existence and this is the primary concept of Advaita metaphysics expressed in different contexts as the essential feature of *Brahman* or *ātman*. Murty has also accepted this specific sense of *sattā* or *viśuddha sattā*, as a part of the definition of *Brahman* and has enumerated in the following lines:

> Though *Brahman* is free from all particulars and limitations (*nirguṇa*) and is *esse purum simplex* (*viśuddha sattā*), the reason for its appearance as many, i.e. *maya* eternally lies in itself . . . while the *definition per essentiam* of *Brahman* is "reality", "knowledge" and "infinity".[19]

Murty also mentions about the degrees of reality and remarks:

> Some thinkers do not admit distinctions in reality — absolute, empirical and illusory existences.[20]

Murty favours the conception of degrees in reality, because degrees in the philosophical conception of reality do not affect

---

18 Murty, op. cit., p. 30.

19 Ibid., p. 4.

20 Ibid., p. 130.

the monistic theory or the idea of pure existence (*sat*). But *pāramārthika sattā* (the absolute sense of reality) does not entertain the degrees or varieties, or any distinction in the conception of reality. *Pāramārthika sattā* signifies the concept of Absolute, devoid of distinction, modification and change. Murty has also used the concept of Pure Being as a substitute concept for *Brahman*, occasionally; and the idea of "being" in Advaita Vedānta means substantial identity amidst the multiplicity of creation to protect the doctrine of monism. The idea of "being" functions as the unitary principles binding all differences together under the notion of "one", the Supreme Being. And this "being" in Advaita terminology is called *sat* or pure existence. Again Murty has used the term Absolute Being to name the totality of facts or existence in Advaitavāda. The main objective of Advaita philosophy is to maintain certain principles of existence which admit all forms; the broad idea of Absolute Being affirms itself and carries the idea of necessary existence, viz. *svayam sampūrṇa*. Needless to say that it is self-determined and it does not refer to any particular existence.

Jñānam (Knowledge)

In the analysis of the concept of *jñānam*, Murty has discussed some significant cognitive issues pertaining to various aspects of the concept of "knowledge"; he has illustrated the meaning and usage of *jñāna* following Śaṅkara's interpretation of the term. Murty has affirmed that the word knowledge while forming the part of the definition of *Brahman* is not the empirical knowledge. Obviously, the concept of *jñānam*, as a defining term, does not imply the distinction of knower, known and knowledge occurring in factual knowledge. The word "knowledge" in the definition of *Brahman* is used as an adjective along with other two concepts — "reality" and "infinity". That is why Murty holds that these three words — reality, knowledge and infinity — are in apposition; reality and knowledge, both of them have been used as the connotation of the term *Brahman*. The word knowledge, when used as an essential feature to *Brahman*, it has to be construed in a special sense. According to Śaṅkara, the concept of knowledge as adjective signifies a different meaning; and in such case the adjectives are specially meant for definition (*lakṣaṇa*) and are not principally meant as grammatical adjectives. Because in common cases adjectives differentiate (*nivartaka*) a thing from other things of its class only, while *lakṣaṇa* differentiates it from all things. Murty cites the example used by Śaṅkara, such as:

> Ether (*ākāśa*) is that which gives scope for extension (*avakāśa pratatā*) as an example of *lakṣaṇa*.[21]

Murty also explains on Śaṅkara's views regarding the application of adjectives to the concept of *Brahman*. According to Śaṅkara, adjectives applied to *Brahman* will be meaningful, only if it is established or well known (*prasiddha*). Śaṅkara also asserts that when the words, reality, knowledge, etc. are used as adjectives, they are principally meant for definition and these words serve to define this meaningful word *Brahman* because:

> A definition would be meaningless if there is no significant definiendum (*lakṣya*); and the word *Brahman* (which is here the definiendum) has got its own etymological meaning (*svārthena arthavān*).[22]

Murty also emphasizes that in the Upaniṣadic definition, the terms reality, knowledge and infinity are not mutually related; each of them is related to the word *Brahman* independently of the others. So, it follows that these attributes of *Brahman* have been used independently in three different senses, in these three forms:

---

[21] Murty, op. cit., p. 61.

[22] Ibid., p. 62.

> Reality is *Brahman*, knowledge is *Brahman* and infinity is *Brahman*.[23]

Murty has pointed out that in the referred quotation, though the concepts of reality, knowledge and infinity are independent of each other, each of them is related to a single concept *Brahman*; each of them comes one after another as an inevitable sequence; the word reality has been used to negate materiality, the word knowledge is used as an adjective along with the other words reality and infinity. The word reality has been used to ascertain the metaphysical sense of the word as different from unreality or change (*vikāra*). Similarly, when the word knowledge is applied to *Brahman*, it signifies that knowledge is an essential feature of *Brahman*. Here, the word knowledge has not been used in the sense of "producer of knowledge" (*jñāna kartā*), i.e. knower, because the knower cannot be real for its changing character. And "moreover, knower implies the distinctions of known, knowledge and knower, and that would contradict the concept of *Brahman* as *Infinite*", that is *Bhūmā* (the vast, i.e. *Brahman*), where no other is known.[24] Murty also clarifies the idea of "knower" as used by Śaṅkara and quotes Śaṅkara's view:

> It is unjustifiable to say that though there is nothing else to be known by *Brahman*, it can know itself, and as such it can be called a "knower"; because if *Brahman* becomes the known, there remains no "knower", as there is no internal difference in *Brahman*. The one *Brahman* cannot be both knower and known, because it has no parts or members.[25]

However, Murty holds that *Brahman* as pure being cannot be known as knower in the ordinary sense and he has exemplified

23 Murty, op. cit., p. 61.

24 Ibid.

25 Ibid.

the meaning of the word knowledge in the definition of *Brahman* in the following lines:

> To conclude, in the definition "knowledge is *Brahman*", the word "knowledge" negates activity, etc. and materiality. To remove the supposition that as knowledge is limited in the world, *Brahman*, which is knowledge, is also limited, it is immediately added that *Brahman* is infinity.[26]

Murty also has mentioned about the anticipation of Śaṅkara that

> *Brahman* cannot be properly signified by the word "knowledge" (*na jñāna śabda vācyamapi tad Brahman*); for "knowledge" is a word which denotes the attributes or modifications of reason (*buddhi*), which are only *ābhāsa* (semblance of *Brahman*). The word "knowledge" cannot signify *Brahman* directly but can only imply it (*lakṣyate na tu ucceyate*).[27]

Because, no words can be applicable to *Brahman*, which have no species, genus, etc. *Brahman* is devoid of all adjectives. That is why Śaṅkara concludes that *Brahman* is unspeakable (*avācya*) and incapable of being the meaning of a sentence, because it is implied to be the substratum of the negation of all duality, while sentences indicate only relations. Śaṅkara, quotes the Upaniṣadic texts:

> From where words return along with mind, and it is indefinable (*anirukta*).[28]

Murty has followed Śaṅkara's conclusive remark that the word knowledge cannot signify *Brahman* directly. But, Murty offers an alternative expression for knowledge, as "eternal infinite knowledge". This phrase seems to follow philosophical code

---

26 Murty, op. cit., pp. 61-62.

27 Ibid., p. 62.

28 Ibid., p. 63.

of language, though there is a logical impropriety. Murty justifies that, by this very impropriety, it serves to show the uniqueness of *Brahman*, and reveals to some extent the mystery of *Brahman*. Finally, Murty accepts Śaṅkara's opinion that the best way of speaking about *Brahman* is the *netivāda* (by negation), for the logic of *netivāda* does not involve any superimposition.

However, in the foregoing account of the concept of *jñāna*, Murty has dealt with the logical conditions of the concept of knowledge, used as a part in the definition of *Brahman*. He specifically maintains that *jñāna* in the definition of *Brahman*, does not signify empirical knowledge; it is pure knowledge characterized as bare awareness (*prajñāna ghana*); this type of knowledge alternatively called *pāramārthika jñāna*, which is identified with Absolute Truth.

Anantam (Infinity)

Murty's interpretation of the concept of "infinity" (*anantam*) is equally remarkable. He has scrutinized the meaning of the words reality and knowledge from logical standpoint. Similarly, he has analysed the logic of the wide term infinity as an essential condition of Advaita metaphysical concept of *Brahman* (the Absolute). In defining the term infinity, Murty also refers to Vedic sentences characterizing the idea of *Brahman*; and he has marked out, wherever the word infinity has been attributed to the concept of *Brahman* to bring out the philosophical significance of the concept of infinity and pointed out its affinity to the idea of greatness of *Brahman*, and how the concept of infinity originates from the attribute of greatness of *Brahman*. Conversely, Murty has also traced out the etymological source of the word *Brahman*, which signifies greatness. This word greatness bears the characteristics of "unsurpassed greatness", no other words can limit that sense and it also indicates that *Brahman* is free from the limitation of finitude, etc. According to Advaitins, the meaning of the word greatness can be understood from the etymological analysis and it also needs amplification. Besides, through the amplification of meaning, we can know more and more about *Brahman*. *Brahman* being the greatest thing of all, cannot have any limitation such as "limited substantiality" and "inertness" and, therefore, is the Highest End. For this purpose of amplification of meaning, Murty has consistently followed Upaniṣadic definition of *Brahman*, and presented the conceptual analysis of these terms *satyam*, *jñānam* and *anantam* keeping in conformity with the scriptural interpretation. Obviously, infinity comes up as one of the basic elements in the metaphysical structure of the Advaita conception of *Brahman*. Thus Murty apprehends that if *Brahman* is equal to the idea of greatness, then the word infinity consistently goes along with the notion of greatness; infinity is inseparable from greatness; finite has limitation and defects, while the word infinite, denies all such limitations. Further, to clarify the meaning of "infinitude", Murty has referred to Śaṅkara's interpretation of *Gītā Bhāṣya*, where Śaṅkara has elaborately discussed this characteristics of *Brahman* as infinite, and that *Brahman* cannot come in the compass of "neither being or non-being". It has already been mentioned that the infinity of

> *Brahman* cannot be described by the word "is", nor by the words, "is not", for as it is supersensual, it is not the object of knowledge in the form "is" or "is not" (*ubhaya buddhi anugata pratyaya aviṣayatvāt*).[29]

Since, *Brahman* is supersensual, it can be apprehended only through the analysis of the meaning of testimony; testimony says that *Brahman* is *great*, it is beyond the range of finite. Therefore, the attributive word infinity follows from the negation of finitude. To sum up: infinity (*anantam*) means vast

---

29 Murty, op. cit., p. 58.

(*bhūmā*), infinity means the *great*, infinity means super-sensuous, pure being; infinity qualifies the metaphysical concept as the highest category. Again, "the word infinity is an adjective by virtue of negating finitude".[30] And, moreover, Murty has repeatedly mentioned that infinity is always used in conjunction with knowledge, and knowledge in conjunction with reality, and pure in conjunction with being. So, infinite is a logical sequence in the order of the attributes of *Brahman*. Besides, the import of infinitude implies the character of *Brahman* as non-relational, unconditional, unlimited, etc. There are other non-relational terms describing these features of *Brahman* such as *nirguṇa, nirākāra, nirlipta* and *niṣaṅga*; all of them follow from the concept of *anantam/anādi*. To say precisely, infiniteness is the logical condition for the notion of eternity. Virtually, the characteristic feature of infinity is to tie up all the attributes of *Brahman* and bring them together under one logical group and it acts as connective, connecting the principal attributes of *Brahman*. Thus, Murty's detailed analysis of the fundamental concepts of Advaitavāda removes the ambiguity of these expressions — "reality, knowledge and infinity". Besides, these concepts represent a comprehensive character of Advaita metaphysics indicating epistemological as well as ontological traits of the system; the word knowledge signifies the epistemological feature, while the words reality and infinity characterize the ontological feature. Indeed, Murty has enlightened the traditional interpretation of Advaita terms in the light of contemporary logical analysis.

Advaita Methodology: Anubhava and Revelation: Analysis

Any philosophical discussion needs a method for the formulation of the problem of concerned topic. Our present concern centres around the metaphysical concept of Advaita

---

[30] Murty, op. cit., p. 62.

Vedānta, *Brahman* the Absolute. I have already discussed Murty's analysis of the concept of *Brahman* on the basis of Upaniṣadic definition of *Brahman* — *satyam, jñānam* and *anantam*. It has been observed that the nature of *Brahman* and the knowledge of *Brahman* are not two different aspects of Advaitism; though they are distinguishable conceptually. In philosophical enterprise, the knowledge of *Brahman* is the ultimate goal of Advaitism. And Murty has contributed a great deal by introducing distinct philosophical methods for the realization of the ultimate goal of Advaita philosophy — realization of *Brahman*. However, I shall confine to two aspects of Murty's analysis of Advaita method — revelation and *anubhava*.

Anubhava

The term *anubhava* is the key concept in Advaita methodology. According to Śaṅkara, *anubhava* of *Brahman* (*brahmānubhava*) means the realization of oneself as *Brahman*. And Murty has introduced this concept as the faculty of understanding the fundamental idea of Advaita metaphysics (*tattva*). He has presented a lucid description of this functional term, *anubhava*. He has also traced out the problems involved in the use of this concept in Advaita thesis on the unreality of world along with the non-dual metaphysical theory. Murty has clarified all sorts of confusions about this term by presenting a detailed account of the function of *anubhava* in acquiring the knowledge of *Brahman*. Murty has sorted out certain cardinal points in the usage of this term in Advaita Vedānta. Sometimes, he has identified *anubhava* with immediate knowledge, in the context of knowledge of *Brahman*. He has used certain cognitive terms for the clarification of the meaning of *anubhava*, since it has been very often confused with mystical experience and the allied area of mysticism. Hence, Murty has included certain cognitive expressions to illustrate the meaning of *anubhava* such as immediate awareness (*aparokṣa dhiḥ*) and immediate knowledge (*aparokṣa jñāna*). Sometimes he has also identified *anubhava* with intuitive expression in the phrases like *sākṣātkāra*, as an integral experience, in which *Brahman* is known as one's self.

However, the prominent feature of Murty's exposition of *anubhava* happens to be remarkable for protecting this notion from Western influence of mysticism, and also distinguishing it from personal religious experience. He states clearly that revelation of *Brahman* is not similar to the experience of a mystic, the concept of *anubhava*, in the context of *Brahman*-intuition (*brahmānubhava*) has been considered as *pramāṇa*, on the basis of Śaṅkara's argument (as presented by Murty):

> Śaṅkara says that as in the case of virtue and duty, scripture alone is not the source of knowledge regarding *Brahman*. To some extent *anubhava* as well as scripture are sources of knowledge regarding *Brahman*, because *Brahman* is an existent thing, and the knowledge of *Brahman* must culminate in experience. According to Śaṅkara, *anubhava* of *Brahman* means the realization of oneself as *Brahman* (*brahmātmabhāva*).[31]

In the first part of his referred book, Murty has explained the function of *anubhava* after Śaṅkara as an essential part of *brahma-jñāna*. He has given many arguments of the Advaitins and put summarily that language cannot account for the ultimate source of creation (*kāraṇa*), the chief cause; because anything that can be said, presupposes "difference", "multiplicity". So he goes ahead in search of different sources of Advaita thinkers and finds out that the "nature of *Brahman*" can be known from the Upaniṣadic statements; and after deep deliberation and intense thought (*Prasaṅkhāyana*, p. 104) on them, knowledge of *Brahman* will be revealed as immediate awareness (*aparokṣa dhiḥ*); *Prasaṅkhāyana* is a necessary course to get direct and

---

[31] Murty, op. cit., p. 112.

immediate knowledge of *Brahman,* i.e. *aparokṣa jñāna* (p. 104), it is an "immediate thing" (*aparokṣa vastu* — p. 107). All these terms qualify *anubhava* as *pramāṇa.*

As a prelude to the fundamental point regarding the knowledge of *Brahman,* Murty presents an illustrative account of the main doctrinal differences among the Advaitins regarding the question of principal means of *Brahman*-knowledge. But he does not adhere to any particular view, rather stresses much upon the conception of *anubhava* which he considers to be the "integral experience", in which *Brahman* is revealed. Murty has reassured that the concept of *anubhava* has been exclusively used in the context of the knowledge of *Brahman.* In the specific sense, *anubhava* of *Brahman* signifies the oneness of *jīva* with *Brahman,* or in other words *jīva*'s realization of *Brahman* (*brahmātma bhāva* — p. 112); this state of *jīva* is known as the state of liberation; there is no gap between knowing of *Brahman* and liberation of *jīva. Jīva* can attain this state after intense deliberation on *mahāvākya*s and *anubhava* is the only means or *pramāṇa* for acquiring the knowledge of *Brahman,* derived from the spiritual texts. And such kind of knowledge has been described as immediate experience (p. 112). This type of experience has also been interpreted by Murty as *anubhava,* along with a sort of conviction, i.e. assured conviction (reasoned conviction). Murty explains this "assured conviction" as the clear undoubted awareness, the awareness of *Brahman,* and such type of experience is generated by the understanding of Vedānta *vākya*s.

Further, Murty extends the meaning of *anubhava* as the resultant, *sākṣātkāra,* i.e. the vision of *Brahman.* But such a type of vision has been well-guarded from the European mystics. Murty clearly says that *anubhava* means a particular mode of mind (p. 115), a faculty of understanding which is radically different from normal way of perception, where perceiving mind and perceiving object are distinct. But all perceptions need not be sense-generated, for perception also occurs in direct cognition, there is a direct cognition of pleasure and pain. Such kind of perpetual knowledge is also a mental mode and it is immediate knowledge of pleasure and pain of which self is directly aware of. This direct awareness of self may be compared to intuition in Western method. But in Advaita Vedānta this faculty of understanding has been illustrated in a different manner, through the example of direct awareness of a person as member of a row, as the tenth man. This is a direct cognition and such knowledge does not contain any supranormal element. Similarly when *jīva* becomes aware of its identity with *ātman/Brahman*, this awareness occurs as *anubhava* or direct awareness. Murty quotes the Advaitic comment on this aspect of *anubhava* as under:

> So too, the knowledge of Brahman is immediate, because Brahman is not different from oneself and a direct cognition of Brahman is not different from the cognition of one self, though the erroneous view of self is removed (as in case of the removal of the 'rope-snake' illusion) by correct apprehension. As Vidyāraṇya said; *anubhava* means a particular mode of the mind, which has for its result the intuition of Brahman.[32]

Here Murty anticipates an argument against the Advaita theory of *Brahman*-intuition as follows; one may suppose that there is the mental mode in the form of *Brahman* and the concept of *Brahman*, "How is then non-duality established by *sākṣātkāra*?" (p. 116). Murty puts forth Advaitin's reply regarding such a possible objection:

> The Advaita school wants to make the point that the knowledge derived from *mahāvākyas* is something like the finger which points to an object, but disappears when that

32 Murty, op. cit., p. 115.

> object itself is perceived. Once *Brahman* is revealed in *anubhava*, all multiplicity comes to an end.[33]

Murty also describes how *anubhava* mediates the relation existing between *Brahman* as witness-consciousness and *ahaṁkāra*, i.e. the individual concept of "I". He resolves this point by pointing out that the Advaitic distinction is necessary for conceptual clarity of *Brahman* as witness-consciousness (*sākṣī caitanya*) and an individual knower — *aham-prataya viṣayī* in Advaita epistemology. Śaṅkara marks out a distinction of *sākṣī* and *ahaṁkāra* signifying the former as class idea reflecting on individual knower, while the latter one conveys the idea of an active agent, doer, enjoyer, sufferer, etc. *Brahman* is pure consciousness without any personal element, it is an impersonal idea and the basis or essence of all individual selves; there is no distinction of knower, known and act of knowing as occurs in factual knowledge. Murty intends to say that *anubhava* brings about the feeling of identity between the individual ego and pure-consciousness. Murty cites an instance to exemplify the *anubhava* of *Brahman*.

> When a pot is known the content of that knowledge is "pot", and knowledge of the pot means awareness of the pot. . . . But the content of the knowledge generated by the Upaniṣads is *Brahman* — Pure awareness. Knowledge of *Brahman* is, in other words, awareness of awareness. When true knowledge of one self arises from the Upaniṣadic sentences, that knowledge (awareness) itself is *Brahman*.[34]

The idea, in the quoted lines, speaks about the awareness of *Brahman* as an awareness of awareness since *Brahman/ātman* cannot be separated from awareness/consciousness. *Cit*/ awareness illumines everything. *Jīva* has to realize the oneness with *cit*/pure consciousness and in this operation, no empirical

---

33 Murty, op. cit., p. 117.

34 Ibid., p. 119.

mode is workable; it is through *anubhava* that *jīva* realizes its identity with *Brahman*.

Murty also discussed certain critical questions about the application of *anubhava* in the context of revelation of *Brahman*. He argues that *anubhava* is not a mystical experience. On the contrary, *anubhava* has to be understood in accordance with the Upaniṣadic idea of "that thou art", because an individual or a personal experience does not count for the knowledge of *Brahman*, much less can it refute scripture. The Advaitins approve that type of experience by virtue of which one can realize the truth taught by the scripture. Murty assumes that *anubhava* has not been used as a mystical experience in usual sense; emotion plays very little part in the Advaita usage of the term. Murty holds:

> It is assurance gained by removing the notions of improbability (*asamabhāvanā*) and contrariety (*viparīta bhāvanā*) from the teaching of Upaniṣads. *Anubhava* is a reasoned conviction arising from deliberation over scriptural texts.[35]

Murty persists his deliberation on *anubhava* regarding the philosophical doubt in the question: "does *anubhava* reveal non-duality?" To get an adequate reply, he intends to study the method of reaching the state of *anubhava*. He has mentioned that the Advaitins, by concentration on "the idea of oneness" and by eliminating external multiplicity, endeavour to divert the minds from all the sense-contents, so that mind may be prepared for the insight of *Brahman* (*sākṣātkāra*) and this state has also been described as *anubhava*. In this state there is no duality between the individual self and the Absolute (*brahmānubhava*). Granting this state of mind as possible, Murty argues that in such intuitions the self does not perceive an Other as the One, but perceives itself as the One.

---

[35] Murty, op. cit., p. 255.

After the discussion on the nature and function of *anubhava*, Murty concludes that *anubhava* (intuition) is not an independent proof for non-dual *Brahman*, because intuitive experience has to be moulded in accordance with the truth taught by the scripture. Śaṅkara never claims that Advaitavāda is based on personal experience, but the Veda is the only source of knowledge in this matter. Murty agrees with Śaṅkara's view that independent personal experience cannot refute the scripture, so also there cannot be only such personal experience as *anubhava* of the "non-dual *Brahman*". However, it is imminent that *anubhava* has no longer been restricted to the experience of seers and sages; rather *anubhava* bears close affinity with the theory of revelation in Advaita Vedānta.

Revelation

Murty in his critique of revelation has pointed out certain philosophical problems of revelation, in the setting of Advaita metaphysics and theology. He has traced out certain vital points of logical inconsistency in the Advaita theory of revelation. Finally, he has ascertained that the Advaita theory of monism cannot compromise with the factors involved in the act of revelation — "the act of revealing" and "something to be revealed". Murty focuses on these two major conflicting issues between the revelation of *Brahman* and the Advaita conception of non-dual *Brahman*, which I intend to discuss. It will be evident from Murty's discussion that *Brahman* cannot reveal itself because of some logical inadequacy in the Advaita theory of revelation. Murty tries to resolve logical problems by analysing all the factors involved in revelation. His main tenet can be brought under the following heads:

1. *Brahman* cannot reveal itself,
2. conception of non-dual *Brahman* is untenable, even if *Brahman* is self-revealing, and

3. manifold world is a necessary requirement for revelation.

Now with this arrangement of data on Murty's critique of Advaita theory of revelation, I shall try to present his views as expressed in his book on the concerned chapter of Revelation. Undoubtedly, Murty, in his critique of revelation, is concerned with the philosophical questions and conceptual analysis of the concept of revelation. Since the concept of revelation is a very important religious concept, Murty could not ignore the religious theory of revelation. But, Murty is primarily concerned with the logical usability of the concept and believes that any theory of revelation derives its sustenance from the logical capabilities of the concept of revelation. That is why Murty examines the conditions of the proper application of concept of revelation, largely in the setting of Advaita metaphysics and theology. The concept of revelation, as displayed by Murty, involves three factors, such as to think of revelation is to think of someone revealing something to someone else. "A revelation without a revealer and a recipient is unintelligible."[36] Now, Murty proceeds to enquire whether the Advaita theory of revelation can fulfil this requirement of three facts — revealer, revealing and revealed — in the revelation of *Brahman*. Evidently, the Advaita monism cannot admit these distinct factors in the revelation of *Brahman*. So, Murty holds that this concept of revelation cannot be applied to monistic metaphysics of Advaita, because according to Advaitin, the highest reality Absolute/*Brahman* is one, non-dual principle which is pure consciousness, an impersonal idea. But the Supreme Reality reveals itself through the evolution of the world. In this regard, the ordering and pattern of events is the revelation of *Brahman*. Murty holds that the metaphysics of Śaṅkara is a strict monistic

---

36 Murty, op. cit., p. 247.

theory, even though Śaṅkara's monism characterizes *Brahman* as self-luminous or self-revealing, and the eternal consciousness (*Brahman*) revealing itself, still the revelation of *Brahman* could not be possible; because there is no one else to whom it could reveal anything. Therefore, Murty ascertains that *Brahman* cannot reveal because Śaṅkara's monism does not admit the reality of two vital concepts — revealer and revealed; there must be three logically distinguishable factors in revelation — revealer, revealing and revealed. Now, it has become obvious that in case of *Brahman*, there cannot be any revelation because *Brahman* also requires a recipient, but there is none.

Murty also argues against the claim of Advaita Vedānta regarding the nature of *Brahman* as self-luminous, i.e. revealing itself in everything. Because in the Advaitic world-view, a recipient of revelation is not available and the world is not real from Advaita philosophical standpoint. Moreover, Śaṅkara has characterized this world as *mithyā*, though *mithyā* does not mean wholly non-existent. Hence, Murty asserts that we cannot conceive *Brahman* as a revealer or self-revealer, because of the Advaitic world-view. Murty's tenet demands the manifold of world as a necessary condition. In the Advaita view, there is no independent status of the world; but it is assumed that the revealer and the revealed are ontologically the same thing. Murty still argues that from ontological point of view, the two cannot be identified because the truth revealed by *Brahman* cannot be said to be identical with any other truth. Assuming that *Brahman* reveals itself in everything, but there is nothing besides *Brahman*, where can it reveal itself? This implies that if *Brahman* reveals itself, it must reveal itself to itself, but it is not a meaningful assertion. So Murty assumes that when Advaitins claim that *Brahman* reveals "itself", it follows that *Brahman* can conceal itself from itself, because revealing something implies concealing something. But it cannot be said that *Brahman* can conceal itself from itself. From this argument, Murty categorically asserts that — self-revelation of *Brahman* has no application in Advaitavāda. Therefore, he ascertains that the concept of self-revelation or self-luminosity is a "pseudo concept". It has also to be noted that in the case of self-revelation, the revealer and the revealed are different things, and the recipient has to be ontologically different from the revealer, but the distinction of *Brahman* as revealer and (world) the recipient of *Brahman* — revelation goes against the principle of Absolute monism.

Murty then proceeds to further elaborate the Advaita theory of revelation in two forms. He has distinctively treated the division of revelation as "general revelation" and "special revelation" tracing out their distinctive features. Murty describes general revelation as that type which indicates the world at large is a revelation of *Brahman*. And, he holds that general revelation in the context of Advaita theory, means the revelation or manifestation of *Brahman* in everything that the world contains. So, *Brahman* (God) discloses itself at different levels through the order of nature. In this sense though, there is a general revelation, strictly speaking it is manifestation or realization; here the supreme is present in its own light (*svaprakāśa*). But Murty apprehends:

> There is a general manifestation of *Brahman*, for all that exists speaks of *Brahman*. But from this we cannot know anything about *Brahman*'s nature, and so it is practically useless.[37]

According to Advaita philosophy, there is also a special revelation contained in the Veda from which we know the nature of *Brahman*. Murty reaffirms Śaṅkara's view that the true knowledge of *Brahman* can be obtained from the Veda alone, because it is impossible to know about super-sensuous thing through our senses or inference, because:

---

[37] Murty, op. cit., p. 271.

> *Brahman* is not a *Deus absconditus;* but is immediately present and self-revealed (*aparokṣa, svayam prakāśa*). In that sense only, there is a general revelation. But from the Veda alone we can know this.[38]

Because, *Brahman* is *śāstraika pramāṇa*, i.e. *Brahman* can be known only through scripture. Further, Murty holds that "unless there is a general revelation, there can be no special revelation".[39] To say otherwise, special revelation implies general revelation and Murty's notion of general revelation is a general one; it is a revelation by God Himself of Himself. Murty confirms that any knowledge of God must be a disclosure by him, since we cannot expect to know him if He is unwilling to disclose Himself. Murty also agrees with Śaṅkara's acceptance of Vedic revelation as the main type of revelation. Veda is promulgated at the beginning of each world cycle by *Īśvara*, and Murty has acknowledged this concept of Vedic revelation. He also admits that "believer in special revelation should have belief that God exists as the revealer", it is a logical requirement for the believer. Murty's point is, belief in the revealer God is derived from the Veda, a revealed text, and Murty makes substantive and comprehensive statement that there is a universal awareness or general revelation of God. Since there is a general revelation by God of Himself all of us believe in God; this is a general revelation. Besides, in elaborating the different factors of Vedic revelation, Murty has discussed different ways of revelation of God such as revelation in religion, *revelation* through *avatāra* and revelation through *anubhūti*. Murty narrates them in accordance with the Advaita view. Revelation in religion occurs in:

> The Veda revealed by God at the beginning of each *aeon* contains the final truth about *dharma* and *Brahman*. When people forget the eternal truth in the Veda, then in order to

---

38 Murty, op. cit., p. 271.

39 Ibid., p. 270.

> put them back on the right path, and reproclaim the law, God incarnates Himself and teaches the quintessence of the Veda. In the *anubhūti* (integral experience) of *Brahman*, which a knower of *Brahman* will have, the real nature of *Brahman* is disclosed.[40]

While discussing the Vedic revelation, Murty has also raised an important question, "what is it that is revealed?" In answering this question he has discussed several types of religious theory of incarnation (*avatāra*) — faith in God, nature and content of revelation. First of all, he has dismissed the *avatāra* theory in Advaita context, because, Śaṅkara cannot accept the theory of *avatāra*; this theory contains the empirical phenomenon of human body, which cannot be identified with *Brahman*, *avatāra* cannot have identity with *Brahman*. Subsequently, Murty holds that religion is not a mere feeling nor emotion. Because the fundamental presupposition of theism is that God is a reality, independent of human subjective feelings. Evidently, religion has cognitive content as it provides knowledge about the Supreme Being and no religion for that matter can be without elements of knowledge. Advaita Vedānta itself claims that valid knowledge (*yathārtha jñāna*) is the means to know the Ultimate Truth; *jñāna* leads to liberation (*mukti*). Murty maintains Advaita tradition regarding the Ultimate Truth as valid knowledge (*yathārtha jñāna*).

Furthermore, Murty asks a pertinent question: "can truth be revealed?" This question is a controversial one because some religious thinkers believe that the revelation consists of information about God, while some other theologians do not accept it. So, the problem seems to be whether God communicates truth, or can it be expressible in proposition? Since there are a series of arguments on framing judgement by divine incarnation, Murty accepts revelation through

---

40 Murty, op. cit., p. 10.

confrontation of the human by the Divine. Murty substantiates his view of revelation through direct disclosure of God and immediate contact with the Divine. He confessed that by devotion, God discloses Himself to the devotee. "God reveals Himself fully only to those who 'appropriate' Him as their father or friend through loving trust."[41]

In concluding remarks, Murty has summed up his views regarding the theory of revelation:

1. First of all, Murty categorically says, revelation is not *sue generis*, i.e. it is not a phenomenon that occurs itself. It is a kind of direct awareness which is essentially similar to our awareness of ourselves and our neighbours; this kind of revelation is general of which nobody is deprived of this revelation. Murty believes that the awareness of revelation implies an awareness of God's revelation, and our awareness of God is His self-revelation. But revelation depends upon the whole activity of man, and presupposes that he can think and will; so human freedom is granted and man is actively receiving and assimilating it. Murty also considers that if we accept a personal God, "who is good and omniscient, and a general revelation, special revelations are intelligible".[42]

2. Murty also claims that revelation must be the revelation of Truth. He concedes that the revealed truth is not the *universal* truth, such as is found in the sciences, but is the *absolute* truth. It is relevant to note that Murty has stipulated a new meaning of the absolute truth:

> Absolute truth is that by which a man lives, and for which he dies, and from which he derives a sense of supreme "repose in being" (i.e. integration in himself

[41] Murty, op. cit., p. 283.

[42] Ibid.

> and harmony with reality). On the other hand, universal truth is relative, particular and obtained by all when they start from finite premises and follow a definite method, and it is expressible in propositions, which are recognized as cogent by all who understand them. On the other hand, absolute truth is the primal awareness of a real presence that confronts man as holy and good.[43]

The sense of *absolute* as implied in Murty's statement indicates that there is a distinction between the concept of *absolute* truth and *universal* truth. Murty emphasizes that revealed truth is absolute to its receiver, though not universal; while scientific truth is universal but not absolute. Regarding the finality of revelation Murty has discussed various senses of the word revelation and accepted that the revelation of God is final. There are various ways of application of revelation, specially, he argues that each revelation is absolute to its receivers. And he firmly maintains that any revelation of God must be final and he offers a very good reason to prove the finality of revelation in this remark:

> . . . if no revelation is final, then we lapse into a state where we are constantly on the lookout for better and greater revelations. . . . It is absolute truth that is revealed in all revelations, "absolute" not in the sense in which various thinkers have used that word while claiming absoluteness for the revelations of their respective religions, but in the sense in which we have used that word (following Jaspers). In this sense, a revelation is absolute only for him who has received it, and for the others who have entered into the same spirit as the original recipient by attuning themselves with the historical consciousness in which that revelation occurred.[44]

---

43 Murty, op. cit., p. 284.

44 Ibid., p. 296.

From the remark of Murty on finality of revelation, it is clear that every recipient's revelation is final to him and "finality" should be understood in different senses. An example may be taken for clarification. The revelation of a prophet of any other religion should be accepted as much absolute as the revelation of the Vedic seers; in both cases, the revelations are considered to be final. This view can destroy the elements of fanaticism. Anyway, Murty has enlightened us with a pragmatic view of the concept of absoluteness. Above all, Murty's deliberation on the Advaita conception of revelation is remarkable for its logical rigour.

Reason

While processing the entire mode of revelation, Murty has referred frequently to the activity of reason as an auxiliary to the process of revelation and analysed rational activity from logical standpoint to determine the valid usage of the term. No doubt, reason acts as a proof in the claim of one's content of revelation, because revelation when expressed in language must be rational in its appeal. Furthermore, reason has to co-ordinate different types of revelation discarding irrational elements in revelation. Murty has laid much importance to reason as an accompanying factor in revelation of God or *Brahman* and hence he considers revelation as higher type of knowledge. He has categorically said that God is postulated by reason on the basis of Kantian analysis. Murty has used Kantian sense of reason as *verstand* (*anumita jñāna*) to substantiate that any revelation cannot be contradictory to reason, though all genuine revelations are above reason. There is also another Kantian sense of reason called *vernunft* which is a metaphysical idea. *Vernunft* is the function of mind, another way of cognition; this usage of reason is similar to Plato's "transcendental feeling". However, referring to these usages of reason, Murty asserts Kantian view that the systematic unity of all knowledge is a *naturale desiderium* of reason and in this sense, reason postulates "that a supreme intelligence has ordered all things in accordance with wisest ends" (p. 327).

> So understood, reason can show that existence of God is a necessary postulate, an implicit belief, involved in all experience. This is not an inferential demonstration, but is nevertheless a valid exercise of mind, a meditation on existence, which shows "(in Luther's words) that the knowledge of God is impressed on the mind of every man by God".[45]

In this remark, Murty has hinted at the significant role of reason in the act of revealing God.

As observed, Murty is primarily concerned with the function of both revelation and reason in Advaita philosophy and theology; he aims at the mutual conformity between revelation and reason. Murty carefully distinguishes between "contradictory to" and "above" reasons, since there is a single term *viruddha* for both of the usages. He makes sincere efforts to remove all sorts of confusion about the meaning of revelation by the application of logic and reason. He has successfully defended that revelation is not wholly different from cognitive and conative processes. He exemplifies how we can possess a new idea, which is not a deduction of previous knowledge, but after "disciplining our natural inclinations and following a search which claims devotion". Murty also supports that religious revelation and creative inspiration, both of them have equal impact on our living; revelation as he holds, works for human problems — in the context of religious truth as well as philosophical truth. Murty has, especially, discussed the method of revelation employed in Advaitavāda of Śaṅkara and compared with Western views to trace out the significant role of revelation in Advaitavāda. As we can see, Murty has never used the word revelation in

---

45 Murty, op. cit., p. 332.

the sense of super-sensible rather that it is accountable in objective language. He acknowledges that both revelation and reason can be made useful to resolve any philosophical problem as occasion demands. Nowhere does he say that revelation is a mere feeling, but revelation contains the elements of reason. There is no antagonism between revelation and reason. Reason and revelation have their respective areas of application and we must know that reason is restricted to certain fields.

It is also relevant to note that reason removes mystical element of human experience. Quite often, confused with the experience in *anubhava*; revelation and *anubhava*, both of them do not occur like mystical events; they are experiences, a sort of celestial pleasure enjoyed by human. Such an experience of revelation is elevated to higher type of knowledge, which surpasses reason and hence, supra-rational, but does not contradict reason. Murty, therefore, assumes that if higher knowledge is possible, it cannot be against logic and reason. Reason, in any case, is the faculty by which man can distinguish between higher knowledge and lower knowledge. Murty admits that in the Advaita system, there is a compatibility between what is higher knowledge and what is rational, logical. Murty also mentions that revelation does not comply with the revealed knowledge of any one chosen man or group of men. In this context, Murty does not entertain the view that Vedas contain the revelation of sages and seers, rather acknowledges that Vedas reveal the ultimate or absolute truth. As we have already noted, Murty recognizes true revelation as general one, or "universal awareness", such as, revelation of God. Thus Murty has completed his deliberation on revelation by compromising between these two faculties: revelation and reason; there is no conflict between these two methods in acquiring philosophical knowledge. He has successfully established the Indian theory of revelation as a faculty of higher knowledge as enjoyed by humans. This Indian approach is more commonsensical, rational and universal in its appeal. In the concluding remark, Murty, quoting Jaspers, makes an emotional appeal "to become authentic men by becoming aware of being; or and this is the something to become ourselves by achieving certainty of God" (p. 332).

Now I would like to present my observations on Murty's review of various aspects of the Advaita philosophy. In the preceding part, I have tried to expound Murty's analysis of fundamental ideas of Advaitavāda. The analytical technique of Murty, conforming to logical rules of language, seems to be irrefutable and his analysis should be adjudged as highly polemical. Indeed, his critique of Advaitism deserves admiration, though I do not agree with his view in many respects. I feel hesitant to point out his initial mistake in employing rules of objective language to the metaphysical theory of revelation propounded by the Advaitins. Murty has made certain tacit assumption that *Brahman* cannot reveal since revelation involves three distinctive phases of action operated through three distinct terms — revealer, act of revealing something and a recipient of revelation. This process of revelation cannot occur by the agency of non-dual *Brahman*, because of the logical inadequacy of the concept of non-dual *Brahman*. Consequently, Murty has condemned the Advaita view of non-duality and assumed that revelation of *Brahman* is incompatible with the indivisible, non-dual *Brahman*. In response to such a radical criticism of Murty, I would like to place my critique of Murty's viewpoint on revelation of *Brahman*. Murty has confused metaphysical theory with objective function of language. But logico-linguistic rules are not applicable to metaphysical issues such as revelation of *Brahman* which virtually talks about the status of the world in Advaitavāda. Murty prefers logical criterion of the term revelation, but the Advaitic revelation enlightens one about the limitations of finite knowledge and helps one attain the state of ultimate reality. In no way, revelation can be deemed at par with formal logical process.

Moreover, Upaniṣadic definition of *Brahman* as laid out in Advaita treatise — *satyam, jñānam, anantam* (truth, knowledge, infinity) — signifies *Brahman* as a qualified metaphysical concept of highest category. It is incoherent to think that *Brahman* should conduct the act of revelation in accordance with the conditions laid by the linguistic usage of the verb "to reveal".

Again, Murty challenges the validity of the basic Advaita ideas such as non-dual *Brahman*. *Brahman* is self-revealing or self-luminous, because these ascriptions are incompetent to explain the theory of creation by way of revelation. This argument may be countered by the instance of sun which reveals itself by way of revealing the objects of the world. So, Murty's argument against "self-revelation" is not conclusive. Besides, Murty's argument, flouting non-duality of *Brahman*, does not affect the oneness of the Advaita conception of reality, since reality is one or non-dual, it is not affected by revelation or non-revelation of it. Revelation may be meaningful in the context of process of metaphysics, while non-dual concept of reality enjoys ontological status in the substantive metaphysics. So, there is no conflict between the two models of metaphysics in Advaitavāda.

Further, *Brahman* is an impersonal concept, the ascription of self-revealing or self-luminous (*svaprakāśa*) connotes to the meaning of *Brahman* as a self-complete idea, this idea belongs to the highest category of reality. The idea of self revelation entails the idea of eternal spontaneity, signifying the ontological status of *Brahman*. Therefore, Murty's analysis of revelation does not adequately address the Advaitic statement: "*Brahman* reveals itself". *Brahman* and revelation are not two different ideas, not that they have been combined to signify an agent and action, that is to say, the revealer revealing on something. *Brahman* need not render itself amenable to the logical conditions of revelation. *Brahman* is an embodiment of eternal revelation revealing everything like the sun; revelation is its natural spontaneous expression. Finite mind, because of its inherent limitations, termed as *avidyā* (nescience), cannot comprehend the infinitude of the Ultimate Reality, which is of the nature of *satyam, jñānam, anantam* (truth, knowledge, infinity).

4

Śaṅkara Vedānta
An Alternative Perspective
— Ganeswar Misra

GANESWAR Misra in course of review of different aspects of Śāṅkara Vedānta, sometimes expressed his notion of philosophical activity. According to Misra:

> The proper business of philosophy is not to propound any theory of creation but to consciously undertake a programme of analytical study of language and meaning, to mark off propositional forms of fundamental types and show their adequacy and ontological implications to analyse the nature and function of discourse and concepts and to assess their capacity to represent reality.[1]

Misra has organized his philosophical programme on Śaṅkara Vedānta in accordance with his utterances in the above-quoted passage. I have also tried to co-ordinate Misra's major works on Śaṅkara's monism for the proper approbation of my review. Misra has undertaken the analysis of Śaṅkara Vedānta from a logico-linguistic, analytical perspective. It brings into focus a novel standpoint from which the methodology, epistemology and metaphysics of Advaita Vedānta can be re-examined. He has thrown search light on three significant concepts of Śāṅkara Vedānta — *śabda pramāṇa* in Advaita method, *adhyāsa* in the

---

[1] G. Misra, *Analytical Study in Indian Philosophical Problems*, Bhubaneswar: PG Dept. of Philosophy, Utkal University, 1971, p. 3.

context of analysis of knowledge and the concept of *Brahman* as *Saccidānanda* in Advaita metaphysics. I intend to present Misra's analytical reflections on these three concepts, collected from his research papers on Advaitism.

Quite significantly, Misra has initiated the discussion with the Advaita method of *śabda pramāṇa*, and my endeavour will be to expound Misra's interpretation of the term along with other allied concepts. Obviously, it will be followed by the analysis of the epistemic term *adhyāsa*. The doctrine of *adhyāsa* as laid by Misra is a logical doctrine employed by Śaṅkara to determine the validity of knowledge and to eliminate all sorts of empirical knowledge, as they involve the violation of logical principle of predication. Consequently, all propositional knowledge has been considered as logically erroneous, and declared as false, which Śaṅkara names *adhyāsa*. After denouncing empirical proposition, Śaṅkara searched for a valid one; successively, he accepted the identity proposition (*akhaṇḍārtha vākya*) as the genuine and ideal form of proposition. Moreover, Misra has pointed out that the identity proposition is devoid of any description leaving no room for pluralism; thus it paves the way for the ontology of monism. Virtually, Misra has analysed the identity proposition to elucidate his thesis on Śaṅkara's logical foundations of Advaita Vedānta. After working out a defence of Śaṅkara's logical theory, I shall underline Misra's significant contribution to the interpretation of three constituent ideas of *Brahman* — *sat*, *cit* and *ānanda*. He has explained the meaning of these concepts to make them intelligible and analysed the fundamental Advaitic ideas in terms of common discourses. To my mind, Misra's critique of Śāṅkara Vedānta can be well understood by the enunciation of the topics chosen for the present work. In fact, Misra has laid much stress on Śaṅkara's critique of language to show how it serves to enquire about the nature of ultimate reality; he has set the ontological thesis of Śaṅkara in the process of the analysis of *adhyāsa* and *akhaṇḍārtha vākya*. Finally, Misra admits that language cannot represent the ultimate reality and reconciles with Śaṅkara's metaphysical conclusion, that *Brahman* is inexpressible in language, i.e. *anirvacanīya*; Misra quoted to textual reference to ascertain the ontological conclusion of Śaṅkara that *Brahman* is the substantive basis of language, i.e. *śabda-mūla*.[2] With a view to develop the full implication of this concept, Misra elaborately discussed Śaṅkara's theory of language or *śabda pramāṇa*.

Method of Advaita Vedānta: Śabda Pramāṇa

Misra begins his philosophical investigation with the method of Advaita Vedānta, viz. *śabda pramāṇa*. He has presented a new interpretation rather reinterpretation of this Advaita methodological concept, *śabda pramāṇa* deviating from the conventional meaning of the term *śabda*. Subsequently, Misra brings about a structural renovation of Advaita Vedānta as a revisionary metaphysical system by way of interpretation of the word *śabda*. I would like to lay out the method of *śabda pramāṇa* as enunciated by Misra. He has often-quoted textual references with Śaṅkara's interpretations on the *sūtras* to stress upon the originality of his reinterpretation of *śabda pramāṇa* as a logical analysis. Obviously, he deviates from the classical interpretation and he has confessed this radical departure from tradition in the following lines:

> But my interpretation presents Śaṅkara as one delighting in the clear light of logical analysis of discourse and this interpretation is in full agreement with his philosophy of language. This interpretation also brings out the full significance of his assertion that reality is *śabda-mūla*.[3]

The quoted passage clearly indicates that Misra pronounces

---

2 *Vedānta-Sūtra* II.11.27: *śrutestu śabda mūla tvat*.

3 Misra, 1971, op. cit., p. 14.

the meaning of *śabda* in clear terms, on the basis of the concept of *śabda-mūla* in the *sūtra bhāṣya*. He illustrates the method of *śabda pramāṇa* as the method of logical analysis of concepts in philosophical discourse, and interpreted meaning of the word *śabda pramāṇa* as critique of language; because the word *śabda* signifies verbal sounds with meanings. Obviously, Misra does not accept the traditional interpretation of *śabda pramāṇa* as scriptural testimony or Vedic authority. Misra tries to confirm that logical considerations conclusively prove that *Brahman* is the substantive basis of language (*śabda-mūla*) and accordingly, Advaita doctrine has been formulated on the basis of critical and analytical study of concepts and discourse, and this logico-linguistic method is the only method for philosophical investigation. He believes that Śaṅkara has followed the method of critical analysis of concepts as signified in the application of *śabda pramāṇa*. Misra also quotes Śaṅkara's version for his claim: "authority has no place in philosophical enquiry".[4] Misra considers this remark of Śaṅkara as authentic and makes this statement as a good ground for flouting classical interpretations of *śabda* in philosophical inquiry. He reinterprets *śabda pramāṇa* as critique of language, and which reveals (a) the falsificatory characters of language, and (b) which informs negatively that, "all that language attributes to reality does not belong to it". Misra summarizes this vital point in a very clear expression:

> This kind of critique provides us with a kind of knowledge, which in the terminology of Śaṅkara is called *śabda-jñāna* and the reality, known through this knowledge, is *śabda-mūla*.[5]

According to Misra, these lines imminently speaks that *śabda*

---

4 *Vedānta-Sūtra* I.1.4, quoted by Misra in *Analytical Studies in Indian Philosophical Problems*, p. 9.

5 Ibid.

pramāṇa is not an empirical method of knowledge like perception and inference, and these empirical methods are not regarded as the proper method of philosophical enquiry; these methods are used for practical purpose. And also knowledge gained through these methods can be falsified by subsequent knowledge. On the other hand, Misra ascertains that *śabda pramāṇa* is the only philosophical method in which knowledge becomes valid on its own right. Misra adds that the author of *Vedānta Paribhāṣā* describes the concept of *śabda pramāṇa* as the "method of logical analysis of the relation of meaning of different words in different contexts". Accordingly, it has been stated that the chapter on *śabda pramāṇa* discusses the question of syntax and meaning, questions of conditions of meaning and meaningful employment of words in the context of significant sentences. Misra, therefore, legitimately claims that the concept of *śabda pramāṇa* does not signify authority or revealed text. So he confirms that philosophical knowledge can be acquired through critical analysis of language and discourse; examination of meanings of words and sentences is the only source of philosophical knowledge.

Misra accepts that empirical methods are useful for practical conduct. On the other hand, the philosophical methods of logico-linguistic analysis lead us to know the structure of the depth of grammar of our discourse. All these programmes in linguistic analysis have been signified in Advaita terminology as *śabda, śruti, āgama*, etc. Misra also argues that all these terms have been used interchangeably by Śaṅkara. Specifically, he persists that *śabda pramāṇa* has been employed by Śaṅkara for acquiring the knowledge of the unqualified, non-dual *Brahman* / Absolute. Moreover, he emphasizes that the proper method of Advaita philosophy is *śabda* (linguistic analysis), which includes some other methodological terms like *śruti* (logical analysis of meaning) and *śāstra* (meaning-rules of language).

Further, he has referred to Śaṅkara's commentary on *Brahma-Sūtra* to reveal the truth that all these terms in the context of *śabda pramāṇa* have been used as a means of philosophical illumination. Again, Misra refers to Śaṅkara's comments:

> *vākyārtha vicarena . . . brahma avagati hi,*
> *na anumanādi pramāṇantara nivṛtta*
> — *Vedānta-Sūtra* 1.1.2

Thus following Śaṅkara's commentary, Misra has explored a new route in the traditional interpretation of the Advaita method of knowledge, as the method of logical analysis of linguistic forms (*śruti pramāṇa*). On the basis of the quoted reference, Misra announces that linguistic analysis is the "be-all and end-all" in Śaṅkara's philosophy:

> *Śabda* and *śruti* univocally signify language and linguistic forms and nothing else.[6]

Misra also ridicules traditional view and remarks:

> The tradition has rendered *śabda* and *śruti* as verbal knowledge but failing to understand its proper significance as logical analysis of language.[7]

In addition, Misra clarifies that the word *śāstra* is synonymously used for the expression "scriptures", and also the conventional meaning of this word *śāstra* has been translated as verbal knowledge gained through logical analysis of language. Thus, according to Misra, the meaning of the word *śāstra* covers two meanings; it signifies scriptural texts (concerning rites and rituals) and in the other sense it conveys the meaning-rules of language. This is how Misra categorically denounces the traditional interpretation of *śabda pramāṇa*. He confidently

---

6 G. Misra, *The Advaita Conception of Philosophy: Its Method, Scope and Limits*, pub. by Shri Biswaranjan Mishra, Utkal University Campus, Bhubaneswar, 1976, p. 10.

7 Ibid.

asserts that Śaṅkara never admitted authority or revealed text as the only source of knowledge; on the contrary, according to Śaṅkara, knowledge revealed through scriptures cannot be accepted as knowledge proper unless it stands the scrutiny of logic and passes the test of conforming to the conventional meaning-rules of language and logic. Misra makes his argument conducive by referring to Śaṅkara's view on this point:

> Right cognition is objective (*vastutantra*) and is not dependent upon scriptural testimony which gives only directions as to what a religious man should and should not do and, therefore, directs man in the matters of religious rituals (*puruṣa vyāpāra tantra*).[8]

He has explained philosophical knowledge as under:

> The knowledge obtained through this source is called knowledge gained through the logical analysis of propositional forms (*śruti jñāna*).[9]

In this quoted statement, Misra confirms that *śruti jñāna* means a kind of knowledge obtained by analysis of meanings of propositions, i.e. linguistic knowledge (*vākya yanitam vākyārtha jñānam śruti*). In this line, it is also implied that *śruti jñāna* is that kind of knowledge, which is not there but which comes up as a sequence of an analysis of meaning-rules. According to Misra, if we analyse the form of statements and pursue the implication of different elements of it, we find the manner of occurrences of these elements in cognitive statement is different. This knowledge of the difference between the two elements (subject and predicate) becomes known by a kind of logical analysis. Besides, Misra illustrates the meaning of the word *śāstra* as conventional meaning-rules of language, which

---

[8] Misra, 1976, op. cit., p. 11.

[9] Ibid., p. 8.

keeps the linguistic forms within the sphere of meaningfulness (*śaṁsanāt kathanāt śāstra*). Further, he adds that in Advaita philosophy the word *śāstra* is derived from the root (*sanas*), which signifies speech. So, he concedes to the view that logical analysis of linguistic forms is the proper method of philosophic knowledge in Śaṅkara Vedānta (*śrutyadayaḥ yathā sambhava iha pramāṇa*). Again, the term *āgama*, as used in Śaṅkara's analysis of knowledge, is also a kind of knowledge derived from the logical analysis of propositional forms. Finally, Misra concludes that *āgama, śruti, śabda* and *śāstra* stand for the logical analysis of propositional symbolism. He wonders:

> how the meditations upon the meaning of the scriptural texts bodily (*anubhavāṅgatva*) enters into an intuitive awareness of God.[10]

Defying the mystical element in philosophy, he argues that logical analysis of the propositional forms in which cognitive assertions are made is the only proper method of philosophical knowledge and the philosophical knowledge can be obtained through the analysis of cognitive forms. He has expressed his view elaborately in the following lines:

> So analysis of the conditions of the different types of discourses and their logic is a kind of study which is philosophically illuminating. This kind of illumination liberates the mind from dogmatic bondage. It is nothing but a dogma to think that all discourses are of one type and their logic and goal are the same. For this kind of illuminating knowledge, analysis of different linguistic forms *śabda pramāṇa* is the only method. That part of Vedic text which are intended to give the knowledge of the ultimate reality or the *Brahman* is objective in character and has nothing to do with moral duties. By studying the pervasive features and the basic assumptions of all objective discourse we find out what is necessarily implied in all such discourses. What

10 Misra, 1976, op. cit., p. 9.

> things actually exist in the world will be known by empirical methods of knowledge like observation, etc. But that there must be a world is known *a priori* by logical analysis of the nature of factual discourse. One can doubt in existence of any particular thing at any particular time, but existence as such cannot be doubted. So the subjective idealist's contentions that all that we are sure of are our ideas is nothing but sophistry. Similarly, any content of knowledge can be doubted but cognition as such cannot be doubted. If I am aware of the presence of a tree at any time I may not be completely sure that there is a tree. But that I am cognizing the world of objects cannot be doubted. A cognizer cognizing things in a world which exists are the two limiting points of the factual discourse. That I am not deluded about my own existence and that it cannot be the case that nothing exists is a satisfaction of the result of systematic doubting. So *sat–cit–ānanda* is all that guaranteed by any kind of factual discourse. This is an eternal truth, which is obtained by the logical analysis of factual discourse.[11]

The above passage reflects a complete review of Advaita method as demonstrated by Misra. In addition, Misra puts forth his idea of Advaitism in contemporary philosophical idioms:

> So, according to the Advaitin, every language has both a surface structure and a depth structure. The surface structure varies in different languages. But the depth structure is identically the same in all of them. To reveal this eternal structure is the aim of philosophy. Logical analysis of language is the only method suitable for this purpose.[12]

Adhyāsa

It is worthwhile to proceed from Misra's analysis of *śabda* to his understanding of the concept of *adhyāsa*. The epistemic

---

11 Misra, 1976, op. cit., pp. 127-28.

12 Ibid., p. 128.

term *adhyāsa* stands *en route* the inquiry of *Brahman* (*brahma-jijñāsā*). Misra views *Adhyāsa Bhāṣya* as an *ab extra* added to the *Vedānta-Sūtra*; in this *Bhāṣya*, Śaṅkara clearly outlines his philosophical programme and gives direction to his method in "absolutely unmistakable term". Misra states that Śaṅkara has enunciated the logical principle of predication on the basis of analysis of factual judgements to determine the validity of propositional knowledge. He also emphasizes that the analysis of propositional/empirical knowledge is the main concern of Śaṅkara in *Adhyāsa Bhāṣya*. So, Misra tries to lay out the principle of predication with reference to Śaṅkara's interpretation of the term. He has demonstrated the nature and function of the fundamental ideas, or the components of proposition, viz. subject (*asmad*) and predicate (*yusmad*) in accordance with the textual reference. With this preview of *adhyāya*, Misra elucidates the doctrine of *adhyāsa* as a logical doctrine to reveal that Śaṅkara is solely concerned with the logical error in factual judgement, in the process of combining two different types of ideas. Śaṅkara categorically mentioned that the logical subject and logical predicate belong to two different categories with distinct and opposite characteristics and their coupling in propositional form is logically erroneous. Our ignorance (*avidyā*) of this category-difference between the two ideas leads to wrong combination of them under one propositional form. In the interpretation of *adhyāsa*, Misra uses symbolic expression for subject as a unique particular (*viṣayī*) and for the predicate, either as sortal universal (*viṣaya*) or characterizing universal. He has illustrated the nature of these two ideas by common examples and exemplified that the particular (*viṣayī*), to which something is predicated, in no way, is dependent on predicate; it can exist without the context of proposition, and in this sense, it is self-complete. Whereas the universal (*viṣaya*) is dependent on the particular, because it cannot convey any meaning without being attached to the particular, and in this sense, it is incomplete, e.g. the statement "am a brāhmaṇa". Moreover, there is no possibility of being mistaken in respect of the particular, while every judgement tends to be falsifiable or corrigible in respect of the predicate, or the universal. From this account of manner of occurrence of the particular and universal, Misra has characterized the particular as "steady, non-fluctuating", i.e. *satya*, and the universal is opposite to it, viz. "unsteady, fluctuating", i.e. *anṛta*. Misra also illustrates the function of the particular by symbolic expressions following Advaita text such as, "I", "it", "this" or "that", all these demonstrative pronouns can function independently without being involved in propositional context; they are constant factors in knowledge; but the predicate, because of its vulnerable character, has been eliminated by Śaṅkara as false ascription. Subsequently, Śaṅkara denounces all propositions, which are counted either as true or false, because of the logical error in conjoining two different types of ideas. Thus Misra confirms that, *adhyāsa* in the context of Śāṅkara Vedānta stands for "the logical error of coupling two different elements of thought with categorial differences of fundamental type". Misra generalizes that every judgement in subject–predicate (S–P) form, on that account, becomes logically erroneous.

Contextually, Misra reviews the traditional interpretation of *adhyāsa* as "superimposition" to show that the doctrine of *adhyāsa* does not describe illusory knowledge like "silver in shell". In a strong language, Misra blames the classical misinterpretation of *adhyāsa* as an act of illusion and he has offered alternative interpretation to this view and pointed out that the illusory examples have been used by Śaṅkara in an illustrative manner, which indicates how a predicate may be misapplied; but it does not mean that whenever a person applies a predicate, he does misapply it. By citing this instance, Misra assures that Śaṅkara is solely concerned with pointing out logical relation among concepts or ideas and not with matters of fact; the very first sentence of the first part of *Adhyāsa Bhāṣya* clearly reads the ideas so far discussed, i.e. "the subject and the object are mutually exclusive ideas, as those of light and darkness", and therefore any type of coupling of them is ruled out from standpoint of logic. Thus, Misra in his self-assertive style concludes that Śaṅkara was concerned with linguistic and logical analysis of concepts and mapping out entire conceptual framework from logical point of view. According to him, Śaṅkara's doctrine of *adhyāsa* preaches a philosophy of language and *adhyāsa* does not hold an account of the illusory character of the world; this doctrine is a case of revisionary metaphysics and not descriptive one.

Misra further elaborates the characteristic of the particular or the subject expression, the point of reference, and he points out that there is no possibility of error in pointing. But in judging this or that, of having this or that characteristic, we may misjudge, because there is a category-difference between the particular and the universal, between the two logical categories of subject and predicate. When we conjoin these two categories of opposite characters, we commit a logical mistake, because differences cannot be identified in one judgemental form. Misra fully agrees with Śaṅkara regarding the category-difference between the particular and the universal as fundamental. Misra ascertains Śaṅkara's interpretations that the particular to which something is predicated is real and rooted in fact (*adhiṣṭhāna*). According to Misra, Śaṅkara's idea of *adhiṣṭhāna* or locus indicates the metaphysical truth of oneness and this substantive idea of locus came out of the analysis of the particular. Misra states more of the particular not only as a locus (*adhiṣṭhāna*), it has a status conceptual system to which universal is always being subscribed; and corrigibility of judgement is due to misapplicability of predicate expression or universal. Evidently, it has been specified that the logical error occurs in the sphere of predication, the logical subject remains unaffected by predication.

After elaborate analysis of the term *adhyāsa*, Misra offers a critical assessment on Śaṅkara's doctrine of *adhyāsa*. First of all, Misra agrees with Śaṅkara's description of the manner of occurrence and the functional difference between the two categories (subject and predicate), but he could not agree with Śaṅkara's view that the two ideas can never be conjoined in propositional context. Misra refutes Śaṅkara's denial on this point, because the logical subject and the logical predicate signify two moments of cognition, there is a category difference between the two in some sense, but it does not mean that they cannot be combined in any judgemental or propositional form and that every judgemental form involves a logical error. Contrarily, Misra argues in favour of the coupling of two different ideas in one judgement, because it helps us to distinguish "the dependent" and "independent" character, "the saturated and the unsaturated character" of the particular and universal, only in the context of propositional form; and their combination can only illustrate their difference. According to Misra, it is rather illogical to say that the two different ideas cannot be combined in one propositional symbolism. In this respect, Misra apprehends that Śaṅkara, like a sceptic, is searching for certainty of knowledge.

All the more, Misra points out that particular in the form of demonstrative symbol like "I", "it", "this" or "that" can never be wrongly used. It is because they cannot be mistakenly used; it is because they are no part of language; they are mere substitutes for physical gesture of pointing at something. So, there is no question of true or false in their usages that may occur in language. In case of purely referring expression, there is no possibility of being true or false since they act as pointers without any descriptive content. However, Misra has expounded the meaning of *adhyāsa* following textual reference and he has rightly observed that Śaṅkara has laid the structure of monism on logical arguments, displayed in *Adhyāsa Bhāṣya*. Misra completes his review with Śaṅkara's remark on right knowledge, i.e. *yathārtha jñāna*, in a very articulated form of language:

> The true cognition, according to him, consists in knowing the *that* by *thatness* alone and not by the *what*. Since, language necessarily employs the class concept; it brings more and more of the *what* to determine the nature of the *that*. Language can give the *taṭastha lakṣaṇa* and not the *svarūpa lakṣaṇa*.[13]

Quite significantly, Misra has enunciated the concept of true knowledge through symbolic expressions of "that" representing the idea of *Brahman* and "thatness" signifying the inherent characteristic of *Brahman* as non-qualified, combined idea of pure existence and consciousness; while *what* signifies descriptive qualities, *that* has no descriptive content, it is pure referring term and a referent can never wrongly refer. No doubt, Misra has retained Śaṅkara's logical reconstruction of the concept of true knowledge (*yathārtha jñāna*), as the significant idea of Advaitism. But Misra could not reconcile with Śaṅkara's elimination of propositional knowledge. He makes a suggestive remark that it is logically illuminating to point out that referring expressions have no descriptive meaning; he also agreed that descriptive words can be misapplied. But, Misra wonders how words with no descriptive context can be examined from logical point of view, because referring words fall outside the domain of language.

Identity Proposition (Akhaṇḍārtha Vākya)

In the analysis of the concept of *adhyāsa*, Misra has shown that Śaṅkara has discarded empirical judgements as they involve violation of logical rules virtually, because of vulnerable

---

13 Misra, 1971, op. cit., p. 6.

character of the descriptive part of proposition. So, Misra takes a transit to the discussion of Śaṅkara's logical theory of propositions. Interestingly, he has noted that Śaṅkara persists in searching out an ideal type of proposition, bereft of any description and devoid of any logical mistake. So, Misra has given an exposition of Śaṅkara's logic referring to Śaṅkara's logical classification of proposition. Accordingly, he has discussed the conditions of relational proposition, i.e. *saṁsargabagahi*; in this form of proposition there are two independent substantives and they are tied up on a relational tie. While another form of proposition asserting an indivisible non-relational meaning is called identity proposition, i.e. *akhaṇḍārtha vākya*, this form of proposition cannot be analysed into two elements of meaning which are tied together. The case of simple identity is asserted in this form "You are That" (*tatvamosi*); this proposition expresses the identity of self which is the final truth. So identity proposition can only describe the reality. Also, identification propositions are self-complete and they express one indivisible meaning, since, two different types of ideas cannot be identified under one form. Śaṅkara accedes to this identity proposition as a genuine form of proposition. Misra takes up Śaṅkara's theory of identity proposition for his discussion in the background of logic of Bradley, to highlight the excellence of Śaṅkara's logic. Misra begins with Śaṅkara's analysis of S–P form of proposition, such as, "the cow is white". This proposition can be taken either in denotation or connotation. If we read denotatively the proposition turns out to be a tautology, since the word "cow" stands for cows of all colours and the word "white" is only a part of the meaning of the subject. If we take the words in connotation, cowness and whiteness which are signified by the words "cow" and "white" respectively, then it will have to be construed as belonging to the same substance. Misra suggests that to account for the unity of meaning of the whole sentence, we have to suppose that this unity is the unity of ground in the same substance (signifying non-duality or Advaita). Misra further clarifies that a proposition is not barely negative in meaning, and the connotative view is preferable; every S–P proposition asserts the identity of subject with differences of quality. Śaṅkara adopts this way of interpretation. This logical theory of propositions, according to which, both subject and the predicate terms are taken in connotation and a reality outside the meaning complex is supposed to be the subject. Following Śaṅkara's theory, the proposition: "this lotus is blue" means, there is an "x" in which "blueness" and "lotusness" go together. Thus Misra illustrates Śaṅkara's theory of subject–predicate proposition where S–P proposition can be shown to be meaningful by reducing them to some form of identity proposition, i.e. the identity of subject with differences of qualities.

Further, Misra points out that Śaṅkara's identity proposition reveals the form of thinking and identity propositions as ideal type of propositions, it is pure and simple, and all other propositions have been treated as their impure forms; an identity proposition expresses an indivisible meaning (*akhaṇḍārtha vākyam*). Misra has referred to the cases of simple identity, found in the typical illustration in Advaita literature, viz. "this is that Devadutta" and "you are the Absolute"; in case of the first illustration as he finds that there seems to be an apparent contradiction (*virodha*), since "this Devadutta" is determined by the *present now* and the *present here*, is different from that Devadutta as determined by some other now and some other here. Hence, Śaṅkara proposes that the true meaning of a proposition can be understood by sublating the determinants and thereby reaching the identity of Devadutta through exclusive as well as non-exclusive metaphorical meanings (*bhāgatyāga lakṣaṇa*). In this illustration "you are the Absolute", "you" in the referred proposition means an embodied spirit and "Absolute" means the universal spirit. Misra points out that in such cases, if we do a way with differences on both sides, we arrive at the identity of meaning which stands for "pure consciousness" or the *unqualified non-dual Absolute*.

In concluding the exposition of Śaṅkara's analysis of the logical form of proposition, Misra points out that Śaṅkara has adopted the metaphysical procedure of searching for one ideal form for all propositions, so that we can know the structure of the world from the structure of thinking. Misra also holds that Śaṅkara's theory of identity propositions is not reducible to attributive ones, and that the attributive propositions become meaningful only when the proposition is shown to assert some kind of identity (identity of subject). Here, Misra brings out the necessary implication of our thinking, i.e. one reality appears in different contexts in changing forms and he intends to show the impossibility of reducing identity proposition to attributive ones while keeping their meaning unchanged. This is how Misra exemplifies that the Advaitic idea that the world is substantially one while different objects are its descriptive forms, which conceals the substantial identity. Misra also compares with Bradley's view, according to which, all propositions are ultimately of the substantive-attributive, and, therefore, Bradley concludes that a monistic universe is the very assumption of a meaningful discourse. According to Bradley, reality is one and multiplicity of the world has got only adjectival status. It is noticeable here that both Śaṅkara and Bradley derived the monistic metaphysical principle on the basis of the analysis of S–P proposition. Misra, therefore, formulates a constructive view that the doctrine of Absolute monism has been derived from the analysis of logical form of proposition. But both the metaphysicians forgot that propositions have no immutable form. In this context, Misra traced out logical criticism of both Śaṅkara and Bradley in the analysis of S–P propositions, because they have assumed that in substantive–attributive propositions, both the subject term and predicate term can be employed in a homogenous fashion, which is not correct. Here, Misra rectifies this point and holds that if both the terms are taken as names of object or names of qualities, then every proposition will amount to an assertion of identity between the subject and predicate or it will be a non-sensical statement like "one quality is another quality". Misra remarks that these philosophers have ignored that in S–P analysis, the subject term is taken referentially and the predicate term descriptively or attributively; both Śaṅkara and Bradley have ignored the fact that substantive–attributive proposition is a genuine type of proposition as it is used normally, and is not tautological. So, Misra urges that there is no need for supposing a reality (in the metaphysical sense) outside the meaning complex as the subject of such propositions.

To sum up, Misra, while expounding the logical theories of Śaṅkara and Bradley, reflects on the difficulties of predication in their logico-metaphysical theories; because their theories lead to assertion that, Reality is the subject of all judgements; and they also conduct the principle of monism in the same way. According to Misra, both Śaṅkara and Bradley hold that Reality is the subject of all judgements because they have not accepted the traditional analysis of S–P proposition. In the traditional S–P analysis both the terms are not taken homogeneously, the subject term is used referentially and the predicate term as descriptively or classificatorily used. For example, "the cow is red", the word "cow" has both a semantical and syntactical function. But both Śaṅkara and Bradley split up the two functions; classify the word in respect of meaning function with the adjective, yet keep the sentence in the subject–predicate forms. The substantive function is assigned to a meaningless symbol "x"; this linguistic innovation misleadingly puts forward the assumptions that "Reality is the subject of every judgement" and that "Reality is indescribable and beyond human thought". This linguistic innovation, according to Misra, accounts for the unintelligible nature of reality.

Misra also finds out another confusion involved in the logico-metaphysical theory because, both Śaṅkara and Bradley make a "mistake of taking" a meaning-relation for a naming-relation. Both Śaṅkara and Bradley assert that in denotative interpretations both the terms of a proposition must name the same sort of individuals, and hence propositional meaning becomes tautological. Misra rectifies this mistake by referring to Buddhists' theory that this difficulty can be avoided if the words are taken in a negative way. Misra here refers to Russell's method of logical analysis, till in the basic proposition, where only one connotative word remains and the subject term is replaced by what he calls "logical proper names".

It is also pertinent to note that Misra does not agree with the entire programme of Śaṅkara, regarding the basic ideal type of proposition which would reveal at once the immutable form of thinking and reality. So, he comments:

> This entire programme of discovering and ontologizing the one immutable form of all propositions is a misdirected programme. Left to themselves propositions have no form of their own.[14]

On the other hand, Misra suggests that we can talk of the relational form of a proposition if it can be shown to be capable of playing its role in the inferential pattern of relational logic. But Misra does not agree that if a proposition plays a certain role in the context of certain inferential pattern, it does not mean that the proposition has that immutable form and that it cannot play a role in any other inferential pattern. So, he considers that this entire procedure of logico-metaphysicians to search out one immutable form for all propositions is a "fruitless process". Misra, therefore, boldly asserts that no

---

14 Misra, 1971, op. cit., pp. 67-68.

philosophical consequence follows from such a discussion on the logical form of propositions. He considers the metaphysical venture as follows:

> Thus, the logical arguments of the metaphysicians are only formal discussions put in a material mode of speech. The metaphysical theories themselves are linguistic innovations. But a linguistic innovation can neither be true nor false. It is not factual either about the world or about the common verbal usage.[15]

All throughout, Misra has displayed the analysis of identity proposition to indicate the process of arriving at the monistic conclusion and this logical demonstration of Śaṅkara is the final proof of oneness of *Brahman*. He has rightly observed that Śaṅkara's logical theory conclusively proves that Reality is the subject and this logical subject is the Absolute/*Brahman* of Advaita Vedānta. He has illustrated how identity proposition only refers to the identity of two referential terms in the form, "this is this", or "that is that", or "I am *Brahman*", etc. Misra has illustrated that all the referential terms used in identity propositions such as "this" (*idam*), "that" (*tat*) and "I" (*aham*) are the expressions used in Advaita literature for the metaphysical concept of *Brahman*. Misra, further, explains that all these demonstrative pronouns stand for unique entities having no descriptive contents. Relational propositions are descriptive and are known as *saṁsargavagahi,* and the proposition where only demonstrative pronouns are used, are called *akhaṇḍārtha vākya* with indivisible meaning. The second type of proposition is self-complete and logical conditions of expectancy (*ākāṅkṣā*) is fully satisfied, which is lacking in the former type of propositions. Misra, therefore, joins with Śaṅkara's view that language is incapable to give the picture of reality and he has expressed this view in clear terms:

---

15 Misra, 1971, op. cit., p. 72.

> One who realizes the oneness of the *Brahman* has to completely give up language. . . . Thus, Śaṅkara's logic leads him to the conclusion that language is incapable of representing the real, that the *Brahman* can be realized only in a state of pure speechless consciousness. All that we know about this *Brahman* is that it is Pure bliss (*self-complete*), and pure existence and consciousness (*sat–cit–ānanda*).[16]

Saccidānanda: An Analysis

Misra has maintained the chronological order in philosophical discussion of Śaṅkara, indicating spontaneous development from the methodology to the setting of monistic theory of Advaitism. We have already been acquainted with Misra's presentation of Śaṅkara's theory of logic and epistemology. Now, we shall try to elucidate Misra's analysis of metaphysical concept of *Brahman*, *Saccidānanda*. Misra, following the philosophical procedure, interprets the meaning of three constituent elements of Brahman — *sat*, *cit* and *ānanda* as "pure existence", "pure consciousness" and "pure bliss", respectively.

Sat

Misra offers an annotation of the word *sat* through the analysis of knowledge, because the true philosophical knowledge aims at discovering the eternal, incorrigible and unchanging ideas as distinguished from the non-eternal, corrigible and changing ideas. He has defined this term with textual reference of *sat*, as that kind of idea which does not change is *sat*, is the eternal (*yat viṣaya buddhi na vyabhi carati tat sat*); "pure existence" is the representative of the idea of *sat*. Contrarily, that kind of idea, which undergoes change is the non-eternal, is *asat* (*yat vabhi carati tat asat*). The idea of *sat* is eternal and can never be absent (*nābhāvo vidyate sataḥ*). He considers that the proper method to distinguish these two ideas, *sat* and *asat*, is the method of discrimination (*nityānitya vastu-viveka*). Misra has illustrated

---

16 Misra, 1971, op. cit., p. 11.

this activity of discrimination between the eternal and non-eternal through the analysis of judgement. He has analysed the various types of empirical judgements to specify the specific function of the subject (*asmad*) and the predicate (*yusmad*) in contemporary idioms. After examining the manner of occurrence of subject of empirical judgements, Misra has assessed how a subject remains as a persistent idea in judgemental knowledge citing a common case of true and illusory knowledge. When we judge rope as snake and subsequently rectify our judgement, it is clear that our mistake occurs in the perceptual object, i.e. the predicate part of the judgement. But the subject (*asmad*) is pure demonstrative symbol, represented as "this", "that", "it" or "I" remains unchanged both in wrong judgement as well as rectified judgement; this instance indicates that there is no possibility of *committing* a mistake in case of identifying a demonstrative symbol. While the predicate part of judgement (*yusmad*) referring to the object of judgement can never be logically certain, as it varies in varied conditions of perception and it is changeable, corrigible, unsteady and, therefore, non-eternal (*anṛta*). According to Misra's interpretation, the subject, as demonstrative symbols is pure referring expression; this demonstrative symbol which refers to the thing signifies "something" which is an unchanging, incorrigible and eternal idea. This is how he has marked out the eternal and incorrigible elements in our knowledge and all these elements are embedded in the idea of *sat*. Misra, to ascertain the function of subject in the demonstrative symbol, refers to Śaṅkara's *Gītā Bhāṣya*:

> The symbol "that" is a universal name, which is applicable in all cases of making statements (*tat pada sarvaṇāma*). Its signification is *thatness*; the knowledge of *thatness* is philosophical knowledge (*tatpada sarvaṇāma, tasya bhava tattva tat viṣayaka jñāna tattva jñāna*).[17]

[17] Misra, 1976, op. cit., pp. 3-4.

This definition implies the nature of the logical subject, as distinct from the logical predicate.

Another eternal and persistent idea, which the Vedāntins have spotted out in our conceptual system, is the idea of existence (*san*). Misra enumerates that the idea of existence is persistent, and it has been identified with the idea of *sat*. He has referred to the Advaita arguments that the existence of objects is variable, for example *ghaṭasan, poṭasan,* etc. But the idea of "existence" is persistent and eternal. So Misra ascertains that the function of logical subject of judgemental knowledge implies this eternal, metaphysical idea of *sat*, which is symbolized by demonstrative pronouns in *Gītā Bhāṣya*. He also affirms that demonstrative pronouns always refer to the point of reference, since the point of reference cannot be wrongly identified; this point of reference implies the idea of existence and again, this idea of existence refers to the subject where a demonstrative symbol is used. On the other hand, which is identified as object may be misjudged; the reference to "something" remains unaffected even by misjudging. So, the idea of existence never fails, though the objects of which the existence is asserted may not be there. Hence, Misra confirms that "the idea of existence and the idea of 'thatness' are not exclusive of one another".[18] Misra exemplifies this statement in this form: "nobody can say that this does not exist". Nor is it significant to assert that "this exists". According to Misra:

> The first assertion is a contradiction and the second is a mere tautology. In the first statement, "does not exist", contradicts what is signified by "that", and in the second, "exist", does the work of "that" twice over. So, the definition of philosophy as knowledge of *thatness* includes in it the knowledge of existence. Philosophy, therefore, is the knowledge of the persistent or the *sat*.[19]

---

18 Misra, 1976, op. cit., p. 4.

19 Ibid., p. 5.

This is how, Misra has described the metaphysical attribute of *Brahman* as *sat* through the analysis of judgement. In the above remark, Misra concedes to the idea of existence (*sat*) as the necessary factor of the philosophical knowledge. He elaborates the function of demonstrative symbol as subject and identifies subject as *sat*; *sat* reflects in every judgement as a perpetual idea. In judging, we assert "something" as existence (*sat*) which can never be falsified, but assertion of the object may be denied. So, "this" as something, being the constant factor of knowledge, has been characterized as eternal, i.e. *sat*. The symbol "this" can never be misidentified or mis-described or misinterpreted, whenever we utter "this", it always refers to something existent. We can never say "this" as something which is not-existent, because that would lead to referential contradiction. The demonstrative pronoun, "this" or "that" or "it" can be used as pure referent without any descriptive content, is an unfailing idea and this idea of pure referent signifies the defining characteristics of *sat*. Misra asserts that *sat* has always been expressed in Advaita Vedānta through referring expressions like *aham*, *idam* and *tat*, and these ideas signify the metaphysical idea of Absolute/*Brahman*.

Cit

Misra has also marked out another persistent idea of awareness/consciousness (*cit*) in knowledge; which also remains steady throughout our cognitive activity, because to assert the existence of anything implies an awareness of it. So, Misra assures that in case of acquisition of knowledge, there is a state of awareness, i.e. *cit*. For instance, when I am aware of a presence of pot, the object may be doubted, but that I am aware of something cannot be doubted. Similarly, the objects seen in the dream are not there, but my dream experiences and my awareness of them cannot be denied. To say that "this is a pot", but "I am not aware of it", is a contradiction in terms. Obviously, to assert the existence of anything is to imply the awareness of it. So, it is undeniable that the idea of awareness (*cit*) is a persistent idea in knowledge. This idea is self-complete and not affected by being attached to the changing objects. Further, Misra clarifies that the idea of mere existence or existence of something without the idea of awareness of that thing becomes meaningless; because the awareness of something accompanies two necessary ideas, existence of something and awareness of that something. Thus, ideas of existence or "thatness" (*sat*) and the idea of awareness (*cit*) accompany each other in any state of knowledge; both the ideas perform same role in knowledge. This combined idea of *sat* and *cit* has been expressed in two different terms, but they cannot be separated. The idea of "this" involves the awareness of "this" too; though *sat* and *cit* are distinguishable ideas, but not separable. This composite idea of *sat* and *cit* is the eternal factor in knowledge. These ideas designate pure reference, pure awareness and self-complete, which are therefore, not affected by being attached to the ideas of changing object. The concept of *sat* which signifies "mere existence" of something is guaranteed by my awareness, *cit*.

Moreover, Misra has referred to Śaṅkara's analysis of "awareness" through the analysis of different states of human experience. Misra explains Śaṅkara's view about human experience and has found out common features of waking experience and dream experience; dream experience is treated as false by the criteria of waking experience. So, it can be said that the existence of object in the dream state of an individual was real while dreaming; experience of dream as a kind of experience cannot be denied; they are treated as unreal in relation to subsequent waking experience. In this context, Misra intends to show the persistency of awareness or consciousness in waking state as well as in dream state. Misra also agrees with Advaitins that the state of "pure consciousness" or "pure experience", even without any reference to object, can never be denied. He illustrates this state of pure consciousness through an experience of "I am aware as such". In this statement, Misra restores that the state of awareness cannot be denied, though objects of awareness can be denied, awareness/*cit* is never dependent on object and, therefore, it is a self-complete idea. Similarly, is the assertion "this is water", in this statement "water" can be contradicted but "something as" "thisness" cannot be contradicted. These two illustrations testify the self-completeness of existence and awareness. Thus, Misra sums up these two ideas of *sat* and *cit* as "self-complete ideas" and compiles self-completeness under the notion of eternal bliss (*ānanda*).

Ānanda

Normally, the word *ānanda* has been used in the sense of "bliss", in philosophical discussion. But Misra defers from the normal usage of this word, in the context of defining characteristics of *Brahman* as *Saccidānanda*. Misra has displayed the role of this word as the unifying factor and signifying idea of completeness (*purṇatā*). The idea of self-completeness or *ānanda* co-ordinates the ideas of *sat* + *cit* (existence and consciousness), under the wide coverage of eternal bliss to bring them together into a required relation and, thus, three constituent ideas form one unitary metaphysical idea of *Saccidānanda*. Misra by linguistic analysis of the concepts of *sat* and *cit* shows their unfailing character and that they can never be misused in language; they never depend upon any other factor for their meaningful expressions. *Sat* and *cit* in Advaita discourse refer to "this" or "that" as an independent expression. Misra, illustrates the logical condition of these two ideas to show that they can never be contradicted in knowledge, and the pure knowledge or pure awareness of "this" is logically certain; that is why, they are regarded as self-complete eternal ideas. Misra explains the idea of self-completeness in his inimical style:

> A completeness, which can neither be increased nor be diminished by the ideas of changing objects, is the idea of eternal bliss.[20]

According to Misra, this "eternal bliss" designates the idea of *ānanda*. Misra believes:

> Philosophy gives the knowledge of "thatness", "awareness" and "self-completeness" as eternal ideas in our intelligible discourse (*Saccidānanda*).[21]

Obviously, Misra interprets "blissfulness" as another name for self-completeness; "thatness" signifies existence (*sat*) and "awareness" signifies pure consciousness (*cit*) and all the three meet the blend in the idea of *Saccidānanda*.

Misra also emphasizes that *ānanda* does not signify pleasure in ordinary sense, on the contrary, it signifies self-completeness. *Ānanda* works for the self-completeness and forms one logical group, containing *sat, cit* and *ānanda* (existence, awareness and completeness). In Advaita terminology, self-completeness has been used for the idea of *svayamsampūrṇa* or *svayamprakāśa*, otherwise called self-luminous. It will be appropriate to quote Misra's interpretations of the concept of *ānanda* in his own language. Misra says:

> Here, blissfulness is another name for self-completeness. It is not in the sense of happiness enjoyed by a person. To say that an idea is self-complete is to say that, it is blissfulness. The word blissfulness is a synonym of self-completeness. Since, the ideas of thatness and awareness are not affected in any manner when attached to "this" or "that" predicate or detached from "this" or "that" predicate, these ideas are complete within themselves. The idea which remains steady within itself and never undergoes any change is the idea of

---

20 Misra, 1976, op. cit., p. 5.

21 Ibid., p. 6.

> blissfulness. Ideas of pleasure and pain are contingent ideas, whereas the idea of blissfulness is eternal, persistent and unchangeable. The ideas of pleasure and pain are not considered here in their subjective connotation signifying pleasurable and painful experiences. They are considered from the standpoint of their logical behaviour as signifying as changing ideas. And experienced pleasure or pain is temporary and changeable. By contrast, steadfast idea which does not undergo any change is said to be a blissful idea. So the idea of thatness, existence, awareness, and completeness all together form one logical group and their steadiness is regarded to be their blissfulness.[22]

It may be noted that the interpretation of "blissfulness" has undergone a revision beyond recognition, the idea of blissfulness has been divested from its usual employment. Referring to its use in Vedānta literature, Misra considers blissfulness (*ānanda*) lying beyond the transitory ideas of pleasure and pain. To clarify the linguistic confusion, Misra warns us that we should not confuse self-complete idea with eternal enjoyment. Because, the word "enjoyment" in metaphysical context may be confused with "eternal enjoyment". So, Misra repeats that blissfulness is just a synonym for self-completeness. To say otherwise, Misra suggests that meaning of these concepts can be understood with reference to the meaning-rules as codified in the doctrine of *śabda*, i.e. *śabda pramāṇa*; it is neither intuition nor speculation that can give us the knowledge of *Brahman*.

It is pertinent to note that Misra has formulated Śaṅkara's doctrine of monism by means of piecemeal analysis of the concept of *Saccidānanda*; *Saccidānanda* is not a name of an entity; the constituent ideas of *sat*, *cit* and *ānanda* are mere persistent ideas as marked out in course of analysis of language. In keeping up the symmetry in analytical activity, Misra has not

---

22 Misra, 1976, op. cit., pp. 6-7.

portrayed the picture of Advaita Absolute as a holistic ideal usually found in the history of Absolute Idealism. His interpretation of the term "Absolute" is illuminating. Misra has illustrated the meaning of Absolute in an ingenious manner. In this context, he has enlightened us through the common use of this word; Misra elucidates the meaning of "Absolute" in terms of common phrases such as "meaning in the absolute sense" and "absolutely speaking about the nature of real". In these instances, Misra intends to show that the word "absolutely" contains an identical meaning despite their grammatical differences.

Misra concludes his critique on Advaita monism adhering to a new notion of the key word "Absolute" in the logico-linguistic style:

> The Absolute does not designate any supra-sensible being, but is only a linguistic correlate in noun form of the adverb "absolutely" in "absolutely speaking". Whatever one says about meaning in the absolute sense or identifying an object in an absolute way, one does not proceed even one step towards proving the existence of anything.[23]

This remark of Misra brings forth the spirit of his philosophical entrepreneurship. Misra is the first Indian philosopher to use the technique of analytical philosophy for the interpretations and criticisms of Advaita Vedānta. In the appraisal of Misra's analytical study of Advaita Vedānta, one has to admit with all admiration that Misra is an original analytical thinker, and that he has analysed the concept of Advaitism in a lucid and intelligible manner. He has meticulously followed the method of contemporary analysis to clarify the nuances and resolve controversies in Advaita Vedānta. In fact, he has traced out several controversial issues in Advaita system and tried to address them with an alternate interpretation.

---

[23] Misra, *The Sources of Monism: Bradley & Śaṅkara*, Meerut: Anu Books, 1986, pp. 128-29.

The foregoing discussions render it absolutely clear that Misra's analysis of Advaita text is a novel academic feat. He looks at Advaita Vedānta altogether from a new perspective; thereby, he shows how the framework being different, the same text reappears with different meaning and message. No doubt, Misra's interpretation is too radical to be received without criticism. It has been aptly said, philosophy grows through debates and refutations. Unlike in the sciences, the problems or issues in philosophy do not have a definite or a conclusive answer. A particular question in philosophy gives rise to a number of answers which are often mutually contradictory or vastly different. This is so, because a philosophical question or issue can be addressed from an alternative framework resulting in the respective solutions. This leaves room for plurality of answers to a singular question. It is no wonder, therefore, that philosophers in their attempt to understand the Advaita text have arrived at different interpretations of it. Fact remains that profundity of a philosophical text consists in the extent, it gives rise to a number of interpretations. Different interpretations of text, by way of refuting each other, do merely shed light on different aspects of the philosophical problem, issue or question. Unlike a scientific doctrine, a philosophical view is neither rendered true nor false. One philosophical interpretation is to be construed as either adequate or inadequate in relation to another. Viewed thus, Misra's interpretation has to be reckoned as novel and innovative. But one may not go along with Misra, when he opines that the classical interpretations of Advaita are inherently erroneous. Rather, every interpretation of Advaita, including that of Misra, should be construed as alternative interpretation arrived at from alternative framework.

Epilogue

Constructive Review

It is said by some scholars that Vedānta is the national philosophy of India. This point needs to be analysed and understood. The literal meaning of the Sanskrit word "Vedānta" is the end of the Vedas (*Veda* + *Anta*); Vedānta means the essence of Vedas. This interpretation of Vedānta presupposes a particular philosophy of knowledge. It is this: the word *veda* means knowledge; the Upaniṣads grew out of the Vedas and the Vedānta contains the essence of both the Vedas and Upaniṣads. The Vedas do not contain any uniform theme nor do the Upaniṣads. Various types of themes, sometimes contradictory and conflicting, are found both in the Vedas and Upaniṣads.

Historically speaking, the Vedānta philosophy, mainly Advaita and Viśiṣṭādvaita owe their origin to *Vedānta-Sūtra* of Bādarāyaṇa (Vyāsadeva). Other scholars of Vedānta have been inspired and influenced by various sources. Śaṅkara is said to be the founder of Advaita Vedānta; Bādarāyaṇa composed the *Sūtra*s and Śaṅkara wrote commentaries. The *sūtra*s are written in an aphoristic style. The first two *sūtra*s such as *athāto brahma jijñāsā* and *janmādyasya yataḥ* are very important in the sense that it speaks out the objective of philosophy and philosophizing, in a nutshell. "What is ultimately real" is the basic philosophical question for Bādarāyaṇa, and *Brahman* is the Ultimate Reality. That from which the entire world flows out is *Brahman*. This statement is concerned with what is ultimately real and it has been one of the main concerns of philosophy both in the East and West. The style of philosophizing through the ages can be classified into the following three types:

1. What is there?
2. How do we know?
3. What do we mean?

As a matter of fact, many philosophers in the past, say for example, Plato, Aristotle, Kant, Kaṇāda and Śaṅkara were philosophizing after the referred models, but differed in respect of their emphasis on one question or the other. In the West, if the pre-Socratic philosophers and Descartes, Spinoza and Leibnitz were busy in finding out the nature of the Ultimate Reality, Kant was keen to spell out the nature of knowledge and how do we know things. On the other hand, the question of meaning became prominent with Wittgenstein, Austin, Ryle and many others.

Let us look at the Vedānta School of thought in general and Advaita in particular from this vantage-point. Bādarāyaṇa, the author of *Brahma-Sūtra*, tried to find out the nature of the Ultimate Reality, in the same manner as the Western thinkers, though he also discussed the nature of knowledge, emancipation and bliss. Śaṅkara, the most authentic and original commentator on it, brought many intricate questions of philosophy into focus. He was not only concerned with what is ultimately real, but also, what is knowledge and how do we explicate it. Further, he did not feel shy of raising questions about meaning or what we mean. In other words, such questions as, "what is real, how do we know and what do we mean" are taken up by Śaṅkara in a most ingenious way. However, this prelude to the concept of Vedānta clearly indicates that Advaitavāda, like any other Indian philosophical system, originated from the *Sūtra* of Bādarāyaṇa. A number of commentaries (*bhāṣyas*) have been written on the *sūtras* and their commentaries as well. This is how, Advaita, Viśiṣṭādvaita, Dvaita, Dvaitādvaita, Śuddha Advaita schools of Vedānta developed in India. Now the question arises: which interpretation or which of the Vedānta systems is appropriate or correct *vis-à-vis* other systems? To answer this question, one has to have a fair understanding of the nature of metaphysics or philosophy. Philosophy is an interpretive inquiry, that is to say, it aims at interpreting seminal philosophical ideas propounded by great thinkers, system-builders and philosophers. In this connection, it may be added that Śaṅkara, Rāmānuja and others have interpreted *Brahma-Sūtra* of Bādarāyaṇa, and other schools have interpreted both Śaṅkara and Rāmānuja. For centuries, scholars have been working on the commentaries of Śaṅkara. In this way, long generation of interpreters set up different traditions of interpretations according to diverse methods of translating Śaṅkara's thought. Swami Vivekananda, S. Radhakrishnan, K.C. Bhattacharyya and some others tried to present a *holistic* or all-inclusive view of Advaita Vedānta. Vivekananda did it to inspire and encourage young Indians. Radhakrishnan and others tried to present an integral view of the same.

As a natural historical sequence, after 1857, three universities were set up in the presidencies of Calcutta, Bombay and Madras; primarily Western philosophy was taught there. Later on, Indian teachers introduced the teaching of Indian philosophy and stressed much on comparative study of philosophy. To name a few, these Indian scholars like Hiriyanna, Radhakrishnan, S.N. Das Gupta, K.C. Bhattacharyya, T.R.V. Murty and many veteran scholars tried to discover intellectual affinity between Indian thought and Western thought. In course of comparative study, they realized the significance of cultural heritage of India and the depth of Indian philosophical systems. It is worth noting that most of the scholars concentrated upon Upaniṣadic thought are culminating in Advaitavāda. G.R. Malkani and K.S. Murty were trained in this line and both of them were well versed in Indian philosophy and Western philosophy. Malkani and Murty studied in India and followed, by and large, the method and technique of interpreting Vedānta in accordance with the principle laid by native scholars, whereas G. Misra went to England in the 1950s and studied with A.J. Ayer. By then, philosophy department of British universities were saturated with philosophical ideas of Logical Positivism and Linguistic-Conceptual analysis. As such, Misra was inspired by the new method and technique of philosophy. Instead of asking the question, "What is there in the World?" Misra asks the question, "What do the statements about the world mean in Advaita Vedānta?". Indead, it was a discovery of Advaita Vedānta by G. Misra. Misra has supported his findings, quoting passages and important statements from scriptural texts. On the other hand, Malkani and Murty followed the traditional path of describing Advaita metaphysical system keeping in accord with their philosophical training. Seen in this light, Malkani and Murty may be placed together as construing Advaita as a metaphysical system. Though there is difference of details of arguments advanced by Malkani and Murty, they have not detached themselves from reviewing Śāṅkara Vedānta as a metaphysical system. Contrarily, Misra has given a new direction to the study and interpreted Advaita applying contemporary philosophical technique. He contributed, absolutely, a new and fresh definition of Advaita and was unique in his constructive interpretation of Advaita. According to him, Śaṅkara, all through his commentary on *Brahma-Sūtra* was engaged in the analysis of language and meaning; the issues raised by Śaṅkara are "linguistic and logical and the solutions offered are logical and conceptual".

Against the above background, I shall try to give an evaluative account of my discussion on Advaita metaphysics in the contemporary perspective. The preceding descriptive part of the theme of work underlies three different types of interpretations, presented by three eminent Advaita scholars — G.R. Malkani, K.S. Murty and G. Misra. I have obtained three valuable models of Advaitic interpretation in course of discussion of the Advaita treatise of those scholars. Now I intend to conclude with a constructive review of the diverse reviews presented in the previous chapters. In accordance with the tune of contemporary thought, I have used symbolic expressions for three models in the following order:

1. review of G.R. Malkani as "theistic monism",
2. K.S. Murty's deliberation on Advaita theory as "critique of non-dualism", and
3. G. Misra's analytical study of Advaita Vedānta as "linguistic analysis of Advaita concepts".

Following this chronological order, I shall proceed to articulate Malkani's review of Advaitism, which perfectly represents the doctrine of theistic monism.

Malkani: Theistic Monism[1]

In my following observations, I shall try to bring out the remarkable features of Malkani's classical interpretation of

---

[1] I have tried to maintain a sharp distinction between theistic monism and theistic religious metaphysics. Theistic metaphysics requires the deity as the metaphysical condition of the system. But a belief in the deity or worship of deity is not necessary. Generally, theistic metaphysics accepts with the specification of characteristics or qualities of deity as the prime concern. Evidently, Malkani's account of Advaitism cannot be counted as a theistic metaphysics of the Western Middle Ages. Malkani elucidates the theory of Advaita religion through the illustration of perfect knowledge and explains the doctrine of Advaitavāda as the synthesis of philosophy and religion.

Advaita Vedānta[2] both as a philosophy and a religion; no doubt, there is a unique blend of philosophy and religion operated by one seminal principle of thought, i.e. pursuance of the knowledge of *Brahman* (*brahma-jñāna* or *pāramārthika-jñāna*). He has successfully restored that the knowledge of *Brahman* is the meeting point of two parallel thoughts, i.e. Advaita philosophy and Advaita religion, against the broad canvas of Advaitavāda. In fact, the metaphysical doctrine and Advaita theology co-operate with each other in moulding a new theory of theistic monism. Malkani has enumerated all the significant features of theism corresponding to the principal idea of monism and composed one unitary idea of Advaitism. All through, Malkani has tried to maintain a consistency in the comparative account of Advaita philosophy and Advaita religion, comparing their points of similarity in the framework of Advaitism. To recollect the salient points of similarity, I would like to begin with the Advaita theory of knowledge and the methodology of Advaita Vedānta exemplified by Malkani. He holds that both the disciplines adopt *supernormal method* and rely upon Śruti and authoritative scriptures as the only recourse to know the Absolute Truth or the Ultimate Reality. Malkani has enunciated the meaning of this metaphysical truth through the analysis of philosophical knowledge, and has also elaborated the religious endeavour in acquiring the knowledge of truth. Subsequently, he has portrayed the picture of God as the shadow of *Brahman* and in this process, the distinction of two concepts such as *Brahman* and God corresponds to two aspects of *Brahman*, i.e. *saguṇa* and *nirguṇa*. Evidently, theistic element lies deep as the inherent characteristic of Advaitism. Consequently, this conjoining of theism with monism of Advaitavāda creates a new model of Advaitin; which I have preferred to entitle as "theistic monism".

---

2 All of my references are to Malkani's book *Metaphysics of Advaita Vedānta*.

Malkani introduces his philosophical programme with Advaita theory of knowledge, because he considers Advaita-vāda as the religion of knowledge. His philosophical entrepreneur is solely based upon the conceptual analysis of knowledge in Advaita; knowledge is the core of Advaita doctrine and both the philosophy and religion in Advaita system strive for one form of knowledge, i.e. the knowledge of *Brahman*, because "to know *Brahman* is to have a life of truth" (p. 6). Further he has ascertained that the knowledge of *Brahman* is the metaphysical truth, and also regarded as the abode of supreme value; religion also shares this common view in respect of the highest goal (*truth*) or the supreme value.

After setting the goal of philosophy and religion, Malkani has to sort out a proper method to achieve the goal, because such type of knowledge can only be acquired through "direct awareness of reality as reality is" (p. 6). This motto guides both the philosophical activity and religious activity in Advaita-vāda. Because of this parity, Malkani holds that Advaita theory of salvation and religious goal are not separate events. Obviously, reason is incompetent to acquire the direct knowledge of the Ultimate Reality. Hence, Malkani approaches to a new method, i.e. the *supernormal method*. Of course, this *supernormal method* has been employed to work for the revealed word or (*śruti*). *Supernormal method* also includes the statements of Upaniṣadic texts. Frequently, Malkani holds that the revealed word is the only authority and the valid source of the knowledge of metaphysical reality, even though it is considered to be super-sensible and non-rational source of knowledge. Again, revealed word is also required in religious discourse; virtually he intends to show that Advaita religion also follows the *supernormal method*. Malkani prefers the expression "supernormal" because it indicates the supernormal way of understanding, since the knowledge of *Brahman* is not a mere intellectual exercise. So, he feels for the necessity of "a method of activating our intuitive apparatus" (i.e. supernormal) (p. 3). This method has been employed in Advaitic metaphysical pursuit as well as in Advaita religion; since there is a close affinity in their pursuit for truth, and Malkani illustrates the theistic element in Advaita Vedānta in the illustrative manner:

> Advaitism may therefore be said to be the religion that seeks perfect knowledge as its goal. It is the religion of knowledge.
>
> — pp. 3-4

Sometimes, he describes Advaitism as the "revealed religion".

Malkani, in consonance with his assertion, analyses the nature of the philosophical knowledge as the higher kind of knowledge and it is identified with Absolute Truth and it can never be cancelled by subsequent knowledge (*abādhita*). Advaita religion also strives for this Absolute Truth and provides remedy for all ills through the knowledge of truth. Further, in the analysis of philosophical knowledge, Malkani addresses philosophical knowledge as the knowledge of ultimate *ground;* Upaniṣadic text describes this *ground* as invisible, supersensible and metaphysical; it is the highest category of reality that underlies all things as the axis of all things and it is the basic truth of all things. This is called by the Upaniṣads as *Brahman*. So, the first stage of knowledge of metaphysical reality is to know reality as the ultimate cause of the world or the metaphysical *ground* of the world; reality is the cause alone and never an effect; it is substantival. All scriptures uniformly agree that *Brahman* is the first cause, the *ground*. In working out the significance of the metaphysical feature of *Brahman* as *sat–cit–ānanda*, Malkani stresses much upon another ascription to *Brahman*, as the *great* and this idea of the *great* is embedded in the notion of *ānanda* (bliss). Scriptures always refer to *Brahman* as *Great Being*, "it" implies broad idea (*bṛhtva*). The *great* is that beyond which nothing can be greater; it is all-pervasive, non-temporal and infinite.

Malkani sums up these two attributive ideas qualifying the metaphysical characterization of *Brahman*. All Upaniṣads also speak about *Brahman* in similar language. Simultaneously, Malkani has restored that the authority of scriptures has given equal status to God as the creator or the *ground*; *Brahman* and God belong to the same category of Ultimate Reality in Advaitism; God is also reagarded as the substantive idea in the causal doctrine. Thus, the knowledge of *Brahman* and God, comprising these ideas of *Great* and *Ground*, has been combined in the notion of the highest value; Advaita philosophy and Advaita religion, both aim at the realization of this ultimate value or the truth. Malkani, therefore, confirms that "philosophy in Advaitism becomes the highest form of religion". Imminently, theistic element pervades in Malkani's account of Advaitism; theism brings out the genuine spirit of Advaita metaphysics.

It is also noticeable that Malkani has portrayed the picture of *Brahman* and God as two corresponding ideas and set them as fundamental concepts in two orders of Advaitism. *Brahman* is at the apex of metaphysical goal, while God occupying the central place of religious goal. Subsequently, *Brahman* and God have been identified with two aspects of *Brahman* — *nirguṇa* and *saguṇa*. In this way, the conceivable states of *Brahman* as *saguṇa* and *nirguṇa* reconcile religion with metaphysics in Advaita Vedānta, the former represents the idea of God in religion, while the latter conveys the Advaita metaphysical aspect of *Brahman*. Obviously, *saguṇa*, primarily, turns out to be the abode of spiritual values since religion is supposed to safeguard the highest spiritual values. But God as *saguṇa* does not belong to the second order of reality. All the philosophical features are summed up in the combined idea of *saguṇa* and *nirguṇa*, combining the Advaita metaphysics with religion. Malkani carefully notes that Advaitavāda does not entertain the idea of *Brahman* with two types of distinctive characteristics. On the contrary, *Brahman* in the state of *saguṇa* becomes functional in relation to multiplicity and it is construed as God; the same *Brahman,* when becomes non-functional, is construed as *nirguṇa*. To say precisely, *saguṇa* and *nirguṇa* correspond to the idea of causal state and non-causal state of *Brahman,* respectively. These two aspects of *Brahman* have been used in two different contexts to signify the two facets of Ultimate Reality; thus God of religion and metaphysical highest being have been identified in the formulation of Advaita doctrine. Indeed, Malkani has maintained uniformity in the analysis of philosophical and religious activities. At the same time, he has marked out a subtle difference between philosophical knowledge and religious faith. Because philosophical knowledge is not mere faith; faith is a transitory state; faith demands to be transformed into knowledge. At this point, Malkani has compromised this point of disagreement and suggested that religious faith should be justified by true knowledge so that it can resume the structure of true knowledge. In other words, faith should be packed up by reason and Malkani assures that faith can be transformed into knowledge. By this way, our intellectual life will not be infected by the subjectivity of faith or belief; we must realize the objectivity of truth. Malkani believes: "this is what Advaita Vedānta enables us to do" (p. 7).

Murty: Critique of Non-Dualism

While Malkani's interpretation of Advaita is predominantly orthodoxical, Murty works out a model of interpretation which appears to be radically antithetical. In a nutshell, Murty's interpretation of Advaita can be seen as a critique of non-dualism. Murty tries to defeat the proponents of Advaita in their own terms. He directs his polemics to show that the concept of Absolute monism is untenable even in Vedāntic framework. The very concept of revelation and *anubhava,* which are taken to be fundamental to Advaita epistemology, is not supportive of *Brahman* as a non-dual entity. Murty's prima-facie rationale behind his criticism is that the very process or act of revelation presupposes at least a revealer and the revealed.

He proceeds to fortify his contention in pointing out that if *Brahman* is the only reality, on account of being non-sublatable, then the world of diversities along with humans and non-humans, including scriptures, will have the status of an illusory reality. While conceding that the scripture is illusory, how can one in the same breath accept that such illusory scriptures yield valid knowledge? Then he goes on to raise a logical objection to Advaitin's tripartite division of reality as it is violative of the law of Excluded Middle. While delineating the ontological status of the empirical world, the Advaitins claim that it is neither real nor unreal; it is neither real like *Brahman* which is unsublatable nor unreal like the fictitious entities such as "sky-flower". It is neither real nor unreal, which are mutually exclusive categories. Thus the ontic status of the world has not been clearly spelt out.

Murty raises another objection with regard to the knowledge of *Brahman*. If *Brahman* is completely real as it is cognized always, the question is — how is *Brahman* cognized? Since *Brahman* is the only reality, only that which is real can know another real. In such a case, there is a semantic oddity, because it would mean *Brahman* knows itself. I cannot say that "I know I", but I can meaningfully say that I know myself because, here, myself is connotative of my thoughts and feelings. It means that for knowledge to take place, the subject must be distinct from the object.

Another objection, advanced against the thesis of non-dualism, is with regard to the locus of *māyā*. If *Brahman* is of the nature of pure consciousness, how can it be the locus of *māyā*? If it conceded that *māyā* is an essential part of *Brahman*, then it can never be annihilated. If the individual soul is thought as being the locus of *māyā/avidyā*, then it has to make room for pluralism. In this regard, Advaitin understanding of *māyā* is *ambivalent*. It can be submitted here that "*Brahman* is the locus of *māyā*" simply means that it has the inherent potency to be mistaken as the world of name and forms. It is to be underlined that *Brahman* does not create the illusion for one and all, it is only the ignorant, who on account of limitation (*avidyā*), mistakes the one to be many. When ignorance is overcome by self effort, *Brahman* is revealed in its own nature.

Non-duality of *Brahman* is again shown to be untenable by Murty from the point of view of *anubhava*. *Brahman* cannot be known through the experience of the multiplicity. Mind has to be divested of all contents so that one can know *Brahman* in its unitary state. Murty argues that even if the mind is completely emptied of manifold sense-content, the fact that there is the intuition of *One*, presupposes the reality of the self other than *Brahman* by which it is perceived. This objection of Murty can be met in indicating the fundamental distinction between empirical experiences which is possible through access to the sense content. On account of the mind's association with the world of particularities, one gets the knowledge of one world which is relatively real. But in the experience of *Brahman* since the multiplicities of sense-content are conspicuously absent, it is not logically tenable to expect the duality between the self (perceiving subject) and *Brahman* (perceived object).

Here the objection of Murty against non-dualism does not seem to have secured ground and shows his reluctance to go along with the Advaitins who moot the thesis that *brahmānubhūti* though a form of experience, it is uniquely distinct from other modes of experience where the subject of experience and the object of experience are distinct. The act of revelation in the process of revelation, the object is *Brahman* and the subject is the finite self. Revelation becomes complete and conclusive only when the finite becomes a part of the infinite (*Brahman*). So, definitionally, the experience called revelation does not leave any room for the dichotomy of subject and object. To suppose that revelation in order to be meaningful must make room for the distinction between the revealer and the revealed amounts to a categorical confusion.

In response to Murty's objection against non-dualism, it is to be underlined that the Advaitins do not commit the logical fallacy of Excluded Middle by viewing the world as neither real nor unreal. The terms, "real and unreal" in the Advaita framework are absolute categories. *Brahman* is real and is absolutely so because given the non-sublability (*abādhita*) as the criterion of reality. *Brahman* is non-sublatable in principle. In other words, *Brahman* can never cease to be real. Sky-flower is absolutely unreal, it can never come into being, as *Brahman* is eternally real and sky-flower is eternally unreal. But when one tries to determine the status of the phenomenal world, it can neither be said to be real like that of *Brahman*, nor unreal like that of sky-flower. The world which is characterized by the presence of diversity is not real, because the sense of diversity disappears when one has the knowledge of *Brahman*. It is not unreal like sky-flower because it does exist, till the point of *Brahman*-realization. So, one can legitimately contend that it is neither real nor unreal without the fallacy of Excluded Middle and both real and unreal, without the risk of contradiction.

The semantic oddity raised with regard to the knowledge of *Brahman* does not appear to be substantive. In case of *Brahman*-knowledge, *ātman* which is essentially *Brahman*, knows its own nature. On account of *avidyā*, the self continues to forget its own essential nature. So, the *Brahman*-knowledge is to be understood against the backdrop of ignorance, whereof the self thought itself to be separate and distinct from *Brahman*.

However, I have tried to respond to Murty's critique of non-dualism of Advaitavāda with reference to Śaṅkara's commentary on *Bhāṣya*. Fact remains that the preceding analysis of Murty's criticism of non-dualism of Advaita does not address all the objections raised by Murty on account of limited purview of the project. Murty directs his polemic at the monism of Advaita from the point of view of the principles of formal logic. Needless to state that rules of logic determine internal coherence and consistency of a system. In other words, given a metaphysical system, the rules of logic can be legitimately employed to being into focus the internal inconsistencies or anomalies in the system, or on the contrary, to show the strength of the system in terms of its being coherent and logically well-knot. A metaphysical system *per se* owes its uniqueness and strength not only to the degree of logical rigour with which the arguments are adduced, but also to the nature of the presuppositions and their explanatory adequacy. Hence, adjudging the merit of the metaphysical pronouncement by means of logic prevents onc from appreciating the very logic of metaphysical exercise. The metaphysician attempts a rational explanation of a reality as a whole, unlike a scientist, who seeks to explain a relative phenomenon in terms of causality. Thus metaphysics, on the one hand, stands conspicuously distinct from science, and in a qualified sense, from the formal logic, on the other. However, Murty's attempt to dish out a critique of non-dualism of Advaita deserves our considered attention because of the new perspective from which the Advaita metaphysics is sought to be viewed. Let me pursue this point still further, stretching out Murty's logical analysis to Misra's linguistic analysis of Advaita concepts.

Misra: Linguistic Analysis of Advaita Concepts

G. Misra, a critical thinker and a questioner, may well have been the first philosopher to use the technique of analytical philosophy for interpretation and criticism of Indian philosophy. Misra's polemics reflect a keen Indian mind concerned with traditional Indian thought and also, profoundly influenced by contemporary Western thinking. He tried to bring about a rapprochement between Indian tradition and Western analytical thought. Although trained in analytic philosophy of logical empiricism and ordinary language analysis, he turned to studying the classical philosophical works of Indian tradition, especially of Śāṅkara Vedānta and employed linguistic method to work out the significance of the fundamental ideas of Advaita Vedānta; he sought hard to sharpen his analytical tools in order to bring out the profound insights of Indian metaphysicians. When he first started this line of thinking, "he was often dismissed as a young rebel, impatient with 'traditional' understanding of tradition" (remark of Jitendranath Mohanty).[3] Virtually, Misra is not a critic of Advaitism of Śaṅkara, but a staunch critic of traditional interpretation of Advaita theory.

In this brief description of Misra's model of Advaitic interpretation, I will only state the main interpretive stance that Misra adopts, particularly, in connection with the Advaita Vedānta of Śaṅkara. In the very beginning, he pronounces his notion of philosophizing. On his view, philosophy, properly speaking, should be a conceptual analysis, and not a psychological account of our experience or advancing our factual knowledge of things. Misra's model is modulated by his conception of philosophy. He extends this conception of philosophy to Advaita Vedānta, and tries to show that "Śaṅkara does conceptual analysis and does not offer either a psychological account of experience or metaphysical knowledge of a transcendent reality", lying behind and beyond the empirical world. No doubt, Misra displays great ingenuity in this interpretive point. Likewise, Misra has worked in different arenas of Advaitism and resolved conflicting issues by the

---

[3] *Language, Reality and Analysis: Essays on Indian Philosophy*, ed. J.N. Mohanty, 1990.

application of linguistic analyses. It will not be possible to lay out the overall views of Misra. But I should note of Misra's ingenious interpretive points of seminal ideas in the deliberation of his research papers.

First of all, I intend to place Misra's renovative thought on the Advaita method of acquiring philosophical knowledge, as propounded by Śaṅkara, which is called *śabda pramāṇa*. It is well known that Śaṅkara regards *śabda pramāṇa* to be a unique source of knowledge of *Brahman*. As it is traditionally understood, this method means that our knowledge of *Brahman* derives from the scriptural text — through the process of hearing (*śravaṇa*), reflecting (*manana*) and meditating (*nididhyāsana*). But, Misra construes *śabda pramāṇa* as a conceptual analysis, whereby one lays bare the presuppositions of meaningful discourse that is the ground of the intelligibility of our conceptual framework. Then, philosophical knowledge is not to be had through any mystical experience; it is not also a speculative proof of any transcendent reality. It is the kind of knowledge acquired by the examination of the "depth grammer" of discourse. According to Misra, therefore, the only suitable philosophical method is the critical examination of our conceptual system (*śabda pramāṇa*). The word *śabda* signifies verbal sounds with meanings. "So examination of meanings of words, sentences, types of sentences is the only source for philosophical knowledge."[4] Here, Misra points out that traditional interpreters have misrepresented the philosophical spirit of Śaṅkara by representing him as an uncompromising dogmatist who finds inadequacy of logical reasoning and, finally, he relies upon the authority of sacred text as an alternative course, for the knowledge of Absolute Reality. But Misra apprehends this assumption as baseless because "according to Śaṅkara, authority has no place in philosophical inquiry" (*Brahma-Sūtra-Bhāṣya* I.1.4).[5] Misra therefore asserts:

---

[4] G. Misra, *Advaita Conception*, p. 16.

[5] Quoted, ibid., p. 9.

> A critical and analytical study of concepts and discourse is the only method available for philosophical investigation. This kind of critique provides with a kind of knowledge, which Śaṅkara calls *śabda-jñāna*, and the reality, known through this knowledge, is *śabda-mūla*. — *Brahma-Sūtra-Bhāṣya* I.1.4[6]

For further clarification, Misra refers to *Vedānta Paribhāṣā* where he finds supportive argument. He cites an instance to show that in *Vedānta Paribhāṣā*, under *śabda pramāṇa*, various types of questions of syntax and meaning have been discussed such as questions of conditions of meaning and meaningful employment of words in the context of significant sentences. Hence, Misra asserts:

> The phrase *śabda pramāṇa* can only and directly signify not authority and revealed text but means of knowledge through critical analysis of language and discourse.[7]

Misra, further, adds that Śaṅkara denounces "extrapolation and negative implication while recommending logical analysis of language the discourse as a whole for investigating into the abstruse matters of philosophy",[8] because "*Brahman* being a non-natural, non-empirical object, cannot be studied by the usual methods of deductive and inductive reasoning useful in correlating and predicting empirical facts".[9] Misra anticipates that Śaṅkara has been misunderstood; because he "condemns" these two kinds of reasoning, hence the interpreters assumed that he must be relying upon the authority of the revealed text. On the other hand, Misra apprehends that Śaṅkara, because of the inadequacy of reasoning, sometimes recognizes intuition (*anubhava*) as an intuitive experience of the oneness of *ātman*. But he clarified that the usage of the word *anubhava*,

---

6 G. Misra, *Analytical Studies*, p. 9.

7 Ibid.

8 Ibid., p. 12.

9 Ibid.

in this context, stands for cognition. But this type of intuitive experience of truth is not considered as *śabda-jñāna*, "*śabda-jñāna* means knowledge gained through the critical study of language".[10] Misra repeats that "Śaṅkara uses *āgama, śruti* and *śabda* interchangeably.[11] However, he completes his findings on the same with an emotional remark:

> . . . . Every language has both a surface structure and a depth structure. The surface structure varies in different languages. But the depth structure is identically the same in all of them. To reveal this eternal structure is the aim of philosophy. Logical analysis of language is the only method suitable for this purpose.[12]

In the presentation of Misra's model of interpretation, I should note another of Misra's ingenious interpretive points on the concepts of *avidyā* (ignorance) and *adhyāsa* (superimposition). A cardinal thesis of Advaita Vedānta is that owing to the beginningless ignorance (*avidyā*), one superimposes (*adhyāsa*) the world of plurality upon the only reality, i.e. the differenceless, indeterminate, one *Brahman*, defined as pure consciousness, existence and bliss. This thesis is understood either psychologically (wrongly perceived) or metaphysically (the one *Brahman* appears as many). Misra refutes both the construals. On his view, the thesis about *avidyā* and *adhyāsa* is a logical thesis, not a metaphysical or a psychological thesis. Misra claims that Śaṅkara has used these concepts as logical tools for the analysis of judgements or propositions. He illustrated the process of knowledge with familiar factual examples, to assert that knowledge is judgemental and "all judgements involve application of concepts" and to know is to be able to apply concepts. But he finds out a logical error in the process because

---

[10] G. Misra, *Analytical Studies*, p. 13.

[11] Ibid.

[12] G. Misra, *Advaita Conception*, p. 128.

> to know is to judge and to judge is to apply a concept, a non-illusory, unreal entity in a beginningless manner. This is technically called *avidyā* or *Ajñāna* in Vedānta literature. So it does not signify a psychological state of absence of knowledge; it only signifies a beginningless process of applying conception in judgemental knowledge.[13]

Misra argues that *avidyā*, which he interprets as the inevitable process of applying unreal concepts in acquiring knowledge, is the cause of *adhyāsa; avidyā* and *adhyāsa* mutually dependent upon one another; *avidyā* is the cause of *adhyāsa*, in the sense of being its logical ground.

Misra also illustrates the concept of *adhyāsa* in an illustrative manner, through the illustration of wrong perceptual knowledge, such as, when we mistake rope for a snake; this is a case of *adhyāsa*, expressed in the form of judgement. In the judgemental analysis, Misra points out that in the words of empirical judgement, there is a wrong copulation, that means, a judgement always joins an idea, meaning or a concept with reality. As example, "this is X", in this form, "this" is a demonstrative which refers to a substance, while "X" is a concept, a descriptive word, a meaning. Thus, judgement combines two heterogeneous elements and the resultant is, therefore, "non-illusory unreal reality". This is a case of wrong knowledge (*adhyāsa*), as interpreted by Misra. Misra also refers to textual reference to explain the meaning of *adhyāsa* as *śatyanr̥temithunīkr̥tya;*[14] this expression indicates that *adhyāsa* is involved in an erroneous process of application of unreal concepts to a reality. He, then, confirms that *adhyāsa* is not a psychological illusion or perceptual error, rather it exemplifies the logical structure of subject–predicate form of judgement. And Śaṅkara discarded all subject–predicate form of judgement

---

13 G. Misra, *Advaita Conception*, p. 87.

14 *Adhyāsa-Bhāṣya* (borrowed from G. Misra's book *The Advaita Conception of Philosophy: Its Method, Scope and Limits*, p. 68).

since they are liable to be false from the logical point of view; and *adhyāsa* is logically untenable because of joining a real with a non-real. So also, the other concept, "*avidyā* is the inveterate tendency to conceptualize".

In a phased manner, Misra begins with an analysis of the subject–predicate form of proposition (I have already appraised of this type of analysis in the concerned chapter on Misra) and then, proceeds to analyse the structure of identity proposition. In this connection, I wish to mention that Misra uses demonstrative pronouns as symbolic expressions for subject, which is called *viṣayī*, whereas the predicate called *viṣaya*, i.e. descriptive content. Here, Misra, after Strawsonean style, has construed the subject *viṣayī* as the particular "this" and *viṣaya* as the universal concept. Misra reversing tradition, replaces *viṣayī*, the subject by indexicals, like "I", and "this", both of them are index words, "non-conceptually referring to a uniquely particular reality"; then, *viṣaya* refers to all universal concepts, descriptive words and general meanings. A judgement combines both and so commits an error called, *adhyāsa*.

But it should not be thought that, according to Misra, Śaṅkara's doctrine of Absolute monism is based upon taking all judgements of subject–predicate form (as the case of Bradley's monism). He carefully guides Śaṅkara's monism to retain the purity of sequence in the formulation of Śaṅkara's doctrine of monism. He offers a detailed account of Śaṅkara's theory of proposition in various forms such as the distinction of judgements as relational and identity judgements. When judgements couple together different elements, known as rational (*saṁsargavagahi*), all subject–predicate forms belong to this group. The other type — identity proposition (*akhaṇḍārthavākyāni*) — is significant to Śaṅkara; identity propositions assert the identity of meaning which excludes all differences, and signifies unity, but are not tautologies; he further elaborates the identification proposition as self-complete, because there is no further expectancies (*ākāṅkṣā*), e.g. "this is this" or "that is that" while there is always an expectancy in the subject–predicate form. Moreover, the descriptive propositions are liable to be erroneous, because there is a possibility of misdescribing and descriptive language by its very nature can never complete its sense, and descriptive proposition signifies plurality. So, Misra has rightly shown that the foundation of Śaṅkara's Absolutism lies not in the subject–predicate analysis of judgement, but primarily, his accords to significant identity judgements. Misra puts up Śaṅkara's view regarding the identity proposition in the following lines:

> Language comes very near to its goal in identification statements. But pure identity can be reached only when language ceases to operate.[15]

Evidently, Misra agrees with Śaṅkara that the Absolute, the *Brahman* is not knowable empirically by descriptive language. Śaṅkara describes the Absolute as inexpressible (*anirvacanīya*). But some of his interpretations of Advaita concepts may be challenged. However, in all fairness to him, I must admit that Misra has suggested new interpretive possibilities for philosophical concepts and any philosophical discussion should entertain new interpretive possibilities. In fact, any philosophical view remains open for an alternative interpretation, revision, modification and even, reformulation; there is no conclusive answer to any philosophical disputes. From this point of view, Misra's analysis of Advaita concepts will continue to be exemplary.

It is pertinent now to conclude by restating the salient points of monism of "Śaṅkara on the basis of my exegesis of the interpretation of Malkani, Murty and Misra. This project has its focus on understanding the Upaniṣadic metaphysics as

---

15 G. Misra, *Analytical Studies*, p. 31.

expounded by Śaṅkara. The monistic (Advaita) interpretation of Śaṅkara has been subjected to critical scrutiny by scholars in the past and in the contemporary times. In order to ensure that the discussion on monistic analysis of Śaṅkara is not diffused, I have restricted my research project to the works of three contemporary scholars — G.R. Malkani, K.S. Murty and G. Misra. Needless to mention that these three scholars introduced to us three distinct perspectives from which the Advaita metaphysics can be reviewed or analysed. The preceding discussions reveal that they do not have a shared point of view, nor can one discover a universal viewpoint from which Advaita text can be interpreted. In course of my analysis of these views, I have sought to show that by and large, metaphysical systems turn out to be logical elaboration of certain presuppositions which are axiomatic or presumed as self-evident. In the foregone discussion, it has been shown how the Advaita metaphysics, as expounded by Śaṅkara, leaves no room for presuppositions, as the metaphysical conclusions in Advaita follow as a necessary result of analysis of concepts.

In course of my study of these three thinkers, I have underlined modest criticism of them in pointing out how in their attempt to provide a new interpretation, they have grown absolutistic in their own ways, by not taking into account the text as a whole. As a result, though their interpretations hold good in respect of some parts of the text, there are certain other parts which prove to be recalcitrant to such interpretations. Fact remains that there cannot be one and only one possible interpretation of a classical text. An original philosophical text always leaves room for alternative interpretations, which indicates that there can be plurality of perspectives from which one can view or review a philosophical text. Multiple interpretations do not undermine our understanding of the text; rather they throw illumination on it from alternative angles.

Bibliography

Adorno Theodor, W., *Metaphysics: Concept and Problems*, ed. Rolf Tiedemann, tr. Edumund Jephcott, Cambridge, U.K.: Polity Press in Association with Blackwell Publishers, 2000.

Allinson, Robert Elliott, *A Metaphysics for the Future*, Aldershot, England: Ashgate Publishing Ltd.; 2001.

Aristotle, *Metaphysics*, tr. W.D. Ross, New Delhi: Cosmo Publications, 2002.

Ayer, A.J., *Language, Truth and Logic*, Pelican Book, 1971 (1st published by Victor Gollncz, London, 1936).

Bhattacharya, Sibajiban and Ashok Vohra, *The Philosophy of K. Satchidananda Murty*, New Delhi: Indian Council of Philosophical Research, 1995.

Das Gupta, S.A.N., *A History of Indian Philosophy*, vols. I and II, Cambridge: The University Press, 1957 (vol. I), 1961 (vol. II).

De George Richard, T. , *Classical and Contemporary Metaphysics*, New York: Holt, Rinehart and Winston, 1962.

Deshpande, Sharad (ed.), *The Philosophy of G.R. Malkani*, New Delhi: Indian Council of Philosophical Research, 1997.

Devaraja, N.K., *An Introduction to Śaṅkara's Theory of Knowledge*, Varanasi: Motilal Banarsidass, 1972.

Drennen, D.A., ed., *A Modern Introduction to Metaphysics*, New York: The Free Press of Glencoe, 1962.

Hiriyanna, M., *Outlines of Indian Philosophy*, London: George Allen and Unwin, 4th imp., 1958.

Lazerowitz Morris, *The Structure of Metaphysics*, London: Routledge and Kegan Paul, 1955.

Malkani, Ghanshamdas Rattanmal, *Metaphysics of Advaita Vedānta*, Amalner (E. Khandesh): The Indian Institute of Philosophy, 1961.

Misra, Ganeswar, *Analytical Studies in Indian Philosophical Problem*, Bhubaneswar: Post Graduate Department of Philosophy, Utkal University, 1971.

———, *Sources of Monism: Bradley and Sankara*, Meerut: Anu Book, 1986.

———, *The Advaita Conception of Philosophy: Its Method, Scope and Limits*, Bhubaneswar: Post Graduate Department of Philosophy, Utkal University, 1976.

Mohanty, A.K., *Upanaisads Rediscovered*, 2nd edn., Bhubaneswar: Elite Publications, 2009.

Mohanty, J.N., *Language, Reality and Analysis: Essays on Indian Philosophy*, New York: E.J. Brill, 1990.

Mukerji, A.C., *The Nature of Self*, 2nd edn., Allahabad: The Indian Press, 1943.

Murty, K. Satchidananda, *Revelation & Reason in Advaita Vedānta*, Delhi: Motilal Banarsidass, 1974.

Passmore, John, *A Hundred Year of Philosophy*, London: Penguin Group, 1ts published by Duckworth, 1957.

Potter, Karl H., *Encyclopedia of Indian Philosophies*, vol. III, New Delhi: Motilal Banarsidass, 1st ed., 1981.

Pradhan, Ramesh Chandra, *Metaphysics*, 1st edn., Bhubaneswar: Centre of Advanced Study in Philosophy, Utkal University, 2009.

Radhakrishnan, S., *Indian Philosophy*, vol. I, Glasgow: Blackie & Son, 1985.

———, *Indian Philosophy*, vol. II, Glasgow: Blackie & Son, 1985.

Russell, Bertrand, *An Inquiry into Meaning and Truth*, Penguin Books, 1940.

Sharma, Chandradhar, *A Critical Survey of Indian Philosophy*, London: Rider and Co., 1960.

Sharma, Pandit Hardutt, *Brahmasutra-Catuhsutri*, Poona: Oriental Book Agency, 1967.

Strawson, P.F., *Individuals: An Essay in Descriptive Metaphysics*, London: Methuen and Co., 1959.

Tarka Vedānta-tirtha, Sri Mohan Bhattacharya, tr., *Bhāmatī*, Calcutta: Kuran Bhattacharya, 1973.

Tarka Vedānta-tirtha, Sri Mohan Bhattacḥarya, tr., *Vedānta Paribhāṣā* Calcutta: Arati Choudhury, Baṅgābdaḥ, 1377.

Tarkabhusan, Pramathanath, tr., *Vivaraṇa Prameya Saṁgraha*, Calcutta: Basumati Sahitya Mandir, Baṅgābdaḥ, 1334.

Thibaut, G., tr., *The Vedānta-Sūtra*, part I, The Sacred Books of the East, vol. XXXIV, Delhi: Motilal Banarsidass, 1962.

Vedantavagish, Pandit Kalivara, tr., *Vedanta Darshanam*, parts I and II (Vedānta-Sūtra), (Shankara Bhasya), Calcutta: Kshirod Chandra Majumdar, 1970.

———, tr., *Vedānta Sara*, Calcutta: The Central Book Agency (6th edn.), Baṅgābdaḥ, 1379.

Wittgenstein, Ludwig, *Philosophical Investigations*, tr. G.E.M. Anscombe, Oxford: Basil and Blackwell, 1972.

———, *Tractatus Logico-Philosophicus*, tr. D.F. Pears and B.F. McGuinness, London: Routledge and Kegan Paul, 1922.

Index